VIRTUAL REALITY

VIRTUAL REALITY

Theory, Practice, and Promise

Edited by
Sandra K. Helsel
and
Judith Paris Roth

Meckler

Westport • London

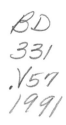

Library of Congress Cataloging-in-Publication Data

Virtual reality : theory, practice, and promise / edited by Sandra K.
  Helsel and Judith Paris Roth.
      p.   cm.
    Includes bibliographical references and index.
    ISBN 0-88736-728-3 : $
    1. Reality.   2. Technology—Philosophy.   3. Computers.
  I. Helsel, Sandra K.   II. Roth, Judith Paris.
  BD331.V57   1991
  302.23—dc20   90-20399
                                                              CIP

British Library Cataloging-in-Publication Data

Virtual reality : theory, practice, and promise.
  1. Technology. Psychosocial aspects
  I. Helsel, Sandra K.   II. Roth, Judith Paris
  306.46

  ISBN 0-88736-728-3

Meckler Publishing, the publishing division of Meckler Corporation, 11
  Ferry Lane West, Westport, CT 06880.
Meckler Ltd., Grosvenor Gardens House, Grosvenor Gardens, London
  SW1W 0BS, U.K.

Printed and bound in the United States of America.

Contents

Foreword

The essence of reality has always been a philosophical puzzle. Semiologists assume that "the universe is as much a construct of man's imagination as it is a brute, concrete reality outside of him" (Hasan, 1984). Anthropologists believe that reality is an intrinsically culturally specific system of meaning that emerges from particular cognitive and social combinations.

Media, particularly image-based media, deepen the puzzle of reality. "The confusion of two-dimensional shadows on the wall with reality is built into film," according to Howard Suber, assistant dean for Film and Television Studies at the University of California at Los Angeles. The Lumiere brothers' 1895 film "The Arrival of the Train at the Station," one of the first black and white films ever produced, caused audience members to jump out of their theatre seats to avoid being hit by the train.

Oxymoronic though the term reads—virtual or artificial reality systems will enable users to become participants in abstract spaces where the physical machine and physical viewer do not exist.

About this Book

Essentially, this book is a republication of articles published in the summer 1990 issue of *Multimedia Review* devoted to virtual reality, a topic that will raise more (and perhaps more significant) questions concerning the nature of reality than the human race has faced to date. In addition, this monograph includes a previously unpublished article dealing with metaphysics, a directory of companies and individuals working with virtual reality concepts and technology, and a suggested readings list not published in the original journal issue.

This monograph begins to explore the complex and multifaceted nature of technologies that will extend the puzzle of reality to questions we cannot yet know to frame. The reader will share the knowledge, the thoughts and dreams, and the minds and voices of virtual reality's pioneers. Contributing authors are scholars, hardware and software developers, educators, information scientists, philosophers, and artists. Most importantly, the cultural assumptions and epistemic categories embedded in the language/thought processes of these pioneers are certain to influence the future direction of virtual reality technologies.

Habermas (1971) pointed out that any technology is invested with ideological orientations. A unique configuration of beliefs and values will be amplified by artificial reality, while other aspects of cultural knowledge will probably be reduced or put out of focus. By bringing together these thinkers, we hope to provide a glimpse of the beliefs and values that will undergird virtual reality.

As for "learning the language" of virtual reality, these authors present comprehensive definitions of the field's inherent philosophies, technologies, and vocabularies. Michael Spring's article "Informating with Virtual Reality" is undoubtedly one of the most valuable resources yet printed for those who desire an intellectual definition of the concept.

It is important that readers become familiar with the breadth of virtual reality systems and the range of meanings, lest the most skilled or most vocal marketers begin to define virtual reality in terms of their own product. There is also a danger that the popular print and electronic press such as MTV, The New York Times, and Rolling Stone—in their attraction to the picturesque—will define virtual reality solely in terms of a single firm, system, or individual.

These essays have been organized into three basic sections: Section I concerns the theory and definition of virtual reality, Section II deals with current applications and development of virtual reality concepts and technologies, and Section III focuses on the promise of virtual reality in a variety of environments—the arts, education, training, and information storage and retrieval.

In Section I, Michael B. Spring examines how virtual reality systems may be applied to certain problems in information science; he offers an analysis of some problems with technology applications in the information science field. In addition, he attempts to define what is meant by the phrase "virtual reality." Myron W. Krueger, often referred to as the father of artificial reality, provides an historical perspective on the development of virtual reality concepts and its windy road to its current state. Michael Heim, a classical philosopher, offers a provocative exploration of the interplay of religion with a virtual reality environment. Heim suggests a contemporary way to establish reality checks for virtual reality systems. He discusses three features of the human existential world (birth/death, leisure time/deadlines, and physical danger) that offer hooks for a real-world anchor. He posits that by building opposite features into virtual reality environments, developers can preserve a contrasting reality check which will preserve the magical atmosphere of VR. In this way, VR systems can continue to engage human imagination over longer periods than if they were simply to reproduce the already given real world.

Section II deals with a variety of current applications and development of virtual reality technologies in both academia and business. Randal Walser from Autodesk, Inc., offers the reader a description of certain virtual reality emerging technologies. Bret C. McKinney, a noted authority on HDTV (High-Definition TV), offers readers an examination of the role these systems will play in virtual reality environments.

His essay includes a brief description of high-definition systems and a glossary of terms.

In addition, Walser describes a cyberspace playhouse under development—"a theatrical medium . . . [that] enables people to invest, communicate, and comprehend realities by 'acting them out.' " Huntley and Partridge from the Computer-Assisted Instruction (CAI) Lab at the University of Iowa describe the development of Fluxbase, an application that integrates the Fluxus art collection with new information storage and retrieval functions using a NeXT workstation. Lastly, Joseph Henderson at Dartmouth College discusses the terms virtual reality and cyberspace, offering a look at the interplay of interactive media and virtual realities actually used in military medical training.

Section III presents several essays describing how virtual reality might be applied in education, arts, and science. Brenda Laurel explores designing virtual reality environments in terms of personal space, theatre, and role playing. Scott Fisher offers an overview of virtual reality environments under development at NASA's Ames Research Center including Jaron Lanier's work at VPL (originally funded by NASA). Fisher describes VIEW, the Virtual Interface Environment Workstation, and its applications in Telepresence (a simulated telerobotic task environment) and Dataspace (advanced data display and manipulation concepts for information management).

The use of computer-generated virtual reality environments for learning and education is explored by David C. Traub within the context of David Perkins' notion of "knowledge as design." In this essay, the author uses Perkins' concept of "the human endeavor of shaping objects to purposes" in terms of virtual reality's "first person" technologies.

We hope this collection of essays will provoke serious reflection by the reader. Typically, we learn by making part of our own understanding the knowledge that is shared by people around us (Vygotsky, 1978). The leaders of virtual reality have shared their knowledge here.

Noteworthy in these chapters is that none of the authors deal with the issue of *perspective.* Given the breadth and depth revealed here, it is remarkable that little consideration has yet been given to viewpoint. For instance, if the History Room in Traub's essay deals with the American Civil War, whose Civil War will be created—the slave, white owner, abolitionist? Will it deal with international and geographical influences? We know from historians that our perspective and understanding of history comes from the historian's viewpoint—what is included, deleted, re-framed, and revised. Many feminist historians assert that written history is history according to white males. How will any individual or group carefully and sensitively, with a deep appreciation for cultural, racial, religious and gender bias, create virtual reality systems?

Moreover, for whom are these systems intended? Timothy Leary among other proponents has expressed the belief that virtual reality will break down barriers between class, race, creed, and gender. Will virtual reality systems be used as a means of breaking down cultural, racial, and gender barriers between individuals and thus foster "human values?" Will virtual reality systems be multicultural in nature or will they only offer Western ways of assimilating knowledge? Will virtual reality systems serve as supplements to our lives, enriching us, or will individuals so miserable in their daily existences find an obsessive refuge in a preferred cyberspace?

Or, will these programs be created for a small, affluent, and well-educated segment of our society already conversant with computer-based technology? Will virtual reality programs offer an escape into the phantasmal for only wealthy citizens?

There are also serious religious overtones when contemplating the concepts of virtual reality and its technology. If we are capable of creating a virtual reality in which all things are perfect, what is the role of God and spirituality? How does humankind (re)define God? Are we re-creating God in a new "form" or are we making God a redundant presence in our personal universe?

These are only a very few of the questions provoked by these thinkers of virtual reality. These chapters and the questions they foster represent only the beginning of an exciting, introspective contemplation of the theory, practice, and promise of virtual reality.

In closing, we wish to state that any technology is an expression of the framework of meaning within which a particular human society lives. Our society is experiencing dramatic changes in terms of demographics and economic stratification. Currently, the world is undergoing enormous change in all spheres of life—political, environmental, intra- and interpersonal, social, economic, religious, geographic, and cultural. The 1990's promise a turbulent, challenging, and hopeful period ahead for all peoples of the world.

What role will virtual reality play in the midst of these changes? In the face of these and numerous other questions, we urge that the tacit, contextual, and metaphorical dimensions of our humanity be honored when the puzzle of virtual reality is pieced together.

Sandra K. Helsel, Ph.D.
Judith Roth

References

Habermas, J. *Toward a Rational Society.* Boston, MA: Beacon Press, 1971.

Hasan, R. "Ways of Saying: Ways of Meaning." In *Semiotics of Culture and Language.* R. Fawcett & M.A. J. Halliday (Eds.) London, Great Britain: Frances Pinter Publishers, 1984.

Suber, H. Interview. *The Anchorage Times* (April 2, 1990; C5).

Vygotsky, L.S. *Mind in Society: The Development of Higher Psychological Functions.* M. Cole, V. John-Steiner, S. Scriber, & E. Souberman (Eds.) Cambridge, MA: Harvard University Press, 1978.

Widman, T., S. Jasko, J. Pilotta, "Technology Transfer." *Howard Journal of Communication,* 1:1 (Spring 1988).

VIRTUAL REALITY

I. THEORY

Informating with Virtual Reality

Michael B. Spring

Zuboff's (1984) studies of automation suggest that even primitive applications of computer technology have the effect of creating alternate, if not virtual, realities for users.

> *In learning to work with this new equipment, it takes a while to believe that when you push a button, something is actually taking place somewhere else. You don't get the feeling that things are connected. How can pushing a button in here make something happen somewhere else.*
>
> *What strikes me the most strange, hardest (thing) to get used to, is the idea of touching a button and making a motor run. It's the remoteness. I can be up in the control room and touch the keyboard, and something very far away in the process will be affected. It takes a while to gain the confidence that it will be OK, that what you do through the terminal will actually have the right effects. (p.82)*

There are a variety of models and tools for interface design. Research on virtual realities is now being added to a mix which includes research on scientific visualization, graphical user interfaces, hypertext, hypermedia, object-oriented programming, and visual languages. These information processing techniques, being applied to the problems of managing the information age are very sophisticated, but they are less than perfectly understood and in some sense still under development. There has hardly been time to deal with the complexities of designing simple user interfaces that work. We still lack rigorous system analysis and design models and software engineering paradigms for designing and building systems with interfaces that make effective use of mice, bit-mapped displays incorporating icons and menus, and high-quality digital signal processing for audio input and output. Developers are still trying to come to grips with the new multi-level complexity introduced by object-oriented systems, particularly for graphical user interfaces and direct manipulation systems. Implementations of hypertext and hypermedia are being explored to determine whether they will constitute new and richer forms for verbal and visual communication complementing the existing standards for oral and written communication. To this mix are added virtual reality systems, systems that use very immediate computer mediation of the sensory and motor activities of the user.

This chapter endeavors to address the question of how virtual realities may play a role in what Zuboff calls "informating."

> . . . *information technology is characterized by a fundamental duality that has not yet been fully appreciated. On the one hand, the technology can be applied to automating operations . . . On the other, the same technology simultaneously generates information about the underlying productive and administrative processes through which an organization accomplishes its work . . . In this way information technology supersedes the traditional logic of automation. The word that I have coined to describe this unique capacity is informate. (1984, pp. 9-10)*

The application of computer technology with the side effect of producing information about the process being automated is one of Zuboff's central themes. Zuboff suggests that this information stream can be made accessible to the user as a mechanism for increasing their involvement in the process.

This chapter examines how virtual reality systems may be applied to problems of interest in information science. It begins by reviewing some of the more interesting virtual reality projects currently underway. This review is by no means comprehensive; it endeavors to provide a flavor of the work based on a review of selected efforts. Then, attention is turned toward defining what is meant by virtual reality. Lastly, we look at an analysis of some problems with technology applications in the information science field.

Review of Selected Research and Development Efforts

Farmer (1988) describes some of the more exciting developments such as VPL's DataGloves and full body DataSuit projects and the NASA

Ames project using EyePhones and VPL's DataGlove to explore various three-dimensional (3-D) worlds such as the space station and the landscape of Mars. He suggests that these efforts have in common two head-mounted TV monitors for stereo imaging, a powerful computer, and a 3-D input device like DataGlove.

In a somewhat more pragmatic fashion, the Media Laboratory at Massachusetts Institute of Technology has demonstrated a number of mechanisms for improving the intimacy of the human-computer dialogue. These include body, eye, and lip tracking mechanisms as well as holographic and stereoscopic displays. As Brand (1987) puts it, "pursuing intimacy and dialogue with computers is what became the connecting idea for the Architecture Machine Group. This continues with the Media Laboratory, for the simple reason that neither subgoal—intimacy or dialogue—has been fully achieved yet, but both remain productively tantalizing."(p. 150) Efforts in the field of animation also need to be considered in a review of virtual realities. The award-winning film *Tin Toy* produced by Lasseter and Reeves of Pixar stands as a landmark achievement in computer-generated imaging. There are other less dramatic, but no less important, efforts in imaging data such as those undertaken in connection with the Infra-Red Astronomical Satellite project. In this case, information about the infrared radiation from stellar observations are made available to scientists in a visual form, allowing them to make judgments about the data more quickly than they might be able to in numerical form. One would also have to consider remote-controlled undersea robots that provide a visual and tactile exposure to deep sea environments for researchers as prototypes for virtual realities. The graphical displays of the U.S. Hurricane Service that allow researchers to visualize the wind speed in hurricanes via color displays may also be considered virtual realities. Recent developments in CAD/CAM and architectural systems that employ computer simulation for users to design and examine products must also be included.

Other efforts, such as ARK at PARC[1] (Smith, 1986), allow the user to engage in "alternate realities" from their vantage point in "meta reality" and to engage in visual experiments that manipulate the laws of nature. At a more human level, the Colab Project, also at PARC (Stefik, 1987), endeavors to provide a virtual meeting environment in a distributed network via public and private work spaces on the participants' screens. Lastly, the numerous object-oriented programming projects (e.g., Cattaneo, Guercio, Levialdi, and Tortora, 1986; Glinert, 1986) that support a graphical user interface may be considered virtual realities.

Fundamental to much of the virtual reality work is research on visualization—"the animated display of symbolic information in the form of concrete objects and physical relations" (Lewis, 1989, p. 1). A review of the current trends and opportunities is provided by the *NSF Report on Visualization in Scientific Computing* (McCormick, 1987) and the follow-up work by the authors (Defanti, Brown, and McCormick, 1989). Lewis (1989, p. 1) extends this thinking more generally into metaphoric visualization, suggesting that "order of magnitude improvements in reasoning can be obtained by transforming unfamiliar situations into familiar ones."

Rohr (1984), Selker and Koved (1988) and others are working to develop standards and rules for the application of visual techniques to information. Chang (1989a, 1989b) provides a model for thinking about the application of visual languages to databases. Crouch (1987) suggests visualization of queries and responses. Korfhage (1986) provides a mathematical model for browsing information spaces.

Considering all these efforts, there appears to be a trend toward nonverbal visual representations. As computational power has increased, so has experimentation with interfaces that provide rich visual information. The terse conceptualization provided by language, found in command driven and verbal display systems is found lacking. Looking forward, a major thrust may be discerned in the development of virtual and metaphoric realities that provide a more direct link between the user and the problem environment modeled by the computer system. Virtual realities will be created for those situations that provide some form of direct or indirect analog-digital-analog experience for users. Alternate realities will be created for those situations that benefit from a rich multi-sensory interface to depict symbolic data or data not available to the human senses.

The Matter of Definition

Webster's Dictionary gives the following definitions for the words virtual and reality:

> *Virtual, "being in essence or effect, but not in fact"*
> *Reality, "a real event, entity, or state of affairs"*

Thus, virtual reality might be paraphrased as "a fact or real event that is such in essence, but not in fact." If the term *virtual reality* is not an oxymoron, it comes very close. In this section, definitions and characteristics of virtual realities are reviewed to develop a means for better understanding what is meant by the term, and how it relates to other aspects of computer and information science.

Farmer (1988) provides a definition of virtual reality systems in describing what he calls cyberspace:

> *Vernor Vinge first described a vision of what might now be called Cyberspace in his novella* True Names *(p.5). The hero of Vinges's story connected to ''The Other Plane'' using EEG electrodes placed on the forehead. The Other Plane was a place where complicated software systems were represented by familiar objects. (p.1)*

Clearly, virtual realities are a type of human-computer interface. Viewed historically, interfaces may be described in three broad categories. In the earliest systems, the interaction was of the form of human manipulation of an inanimate object. The computer was very much a simple and straightforward machine that carried out repetitive operations understandable to humans but at a higher speed. Early computational problems were characteristic of this era. The interaction, if elevated to that level, was little more than the provision of an explicit instruction set to be carried out without deviation. The interaction was such that all control resided with the user.

In the second era is the development of a dialogue between the user and the system. System designers worked to impart some level of intelligence and control to the system to enable this dialogue with the user. In primitive forms, a simple context sensitive help system is an example of such an effort. More sophisticated efforts in expert system design typify this stage. Control is now shared with the computer. As the systems got "more intelligent,"[2] control was shared more equally and indeed in some situations some users even believed that more control resided with the computer, based on better knowledge representations and more sophisticated production rules in selected areas.

In the third era of human-machine interfaces, the constructed system emulates a particular environment. Perhaps the first crude prototype of such a system was the Xerox STAR (Smith, 1982).[3] In these cases, the system is constructed with rules and knowledge about "reality." For the first time, systems were designed where control of the situation was, in part, outside the realm of the human-computer dialogue. A very simple example of such a rule is demonstrated by the move command on the STAR. In that environment, the move command has the impact of causing an object to be moved from one locality to another, e.g., a desktop to a file service. However, the system will not move an object to the printer, but instead copies it to save the user from losing the electronic copy. Thus, the system ignores the user command and takes a responsive but nonetheless different action. The ultimate form of this level of human-computer interaction may be depicted by the Holodeck simulations from the television series *Star Trek: The Next Generation.* Here the system, once started, views the user as only one data source and, with the exception of an override command, not as the most dominant force in the control of the developed interaction.

In a broad historical perspective, virtual realities may be classed as a form of interface characterized by an environmental simulation controlled only in part by the user. Virtual realities represent a natural evolution of interface design with increasing control of the interface being placed with the computer system.

In addition to the dimension of interaction control, virtual realities may be characterized by the nature of the reality being depicted. As suggested in the review, work currently in progress falls on a continuum from the development of computer-mediated realities to computer-developed alternate realities. Efforts such as remote-controlled undersea or interplanetary robots provide computer-mediated realities. Moving along the continuum are such efforts (e.g., NASA Ames Mars project) that have a data source based in reality—the Viking data that forms the basis of the visualization—but that allow the user to experience a reality that is not really happening. Moving further, many of the CAD/CAM and other design efforts allow for exposure to a constructed reality that is possible but not actual. This is best typified by the NASA-AMES space station effort and some of the architectural simulations. Finally, at the far end of the continuum are efforts such as ARK or the microworld learning environments. In these situations, the laws that govern the universe as we know it may be modified, suspended, or contradicted, potentially under the control of the user. What is experienced is less reality, or virtual reality, and more some form of alternate reality.

A third characteristic of virtual realities is the *naturalness* of user involvement in the reality. One imagines cyberspace or the Star Trek Holodeck to be virtual realities that are indistinguishable from reality. In working projects, these effects are achieved by devices such as Eyephones and DataGloves. Clearly, the VPL experiments allow for a greater degree of user involvement than do CRT-based realities in which the user imagines cursor or mouse movements to be the equivalent of some other bodily movement as is the case with Microsoft's Flight Simulator.

Thus, interface design is the broad context for virtual reality efforts. Control factors, reality base, and naturalness of user involvement provide three dimensions for the classification of efforts as shown in Figure 1. Whether another context and other dimensions might better define the various efforts is a matter that will only become clear with further experimentation. For purposes of discussion, this classification will suffice. Two classes of virtual reality projects are plotted against these dimensions depicted as a cube in Figure 2. The microworld types of projects are generally limited in how they accept user input, provide access to and control of "reality," and are governed by the rules set down for the system as well as the user. In contrast, remote-controlled sensing devices are more user-controlled, provide access to reality as we know it, and provide a spectrum of involvement mechanisms that run the gamut from primitive computer controls to naturalistic extensions of human action.

Issues for Virtual Reality Work in Information Science

Farmer (1988) identifies several issues of concern for the development of virtual realities. His concern is primarily with the development of alternate virtual realities by multiple users for entertainment purposes. He identifies issues such as graphic resolution and user interface standards, data communications standards, and CPU power. These same concerns exist for the development of virtual reality interfaces for the information field, but there are other significant issues as well.

From the perspective of information science, three issues have to be addressed:

1. The volume of information data
2. The types of data or information
3. The relationships between the data or information.

In large part, virtual reality projects address the issue of analog signal acquisition, digitization, mediation, and presentation. In information science, sources include not only signals, but data[4] and information.[5] These various "data" types, their extent or volume, and the fact that pieces of information may relate all form important concerns for information science when considering interface design.

Information science must address the development of interfaces for voluminous data collections, such as a high-resolution spy satellite which gathers data at a much higher rate than is manageable by a single human. Information systems mediate signals and higher aggregate levels of signals, such as data and information; so while visualizing 100,000 customer ratings of automobile quality on a five-point rating scale is one thing, visualizing the written comments of the same 100,000 customers may be considerably more difficult. Finally, there are problems associated with the fact that non-contingent pieces of information presented may be connected without using easily understood terms, e.g., in listening to a speech, the auditory signals are connected by temporal continuity, but the parts of information presented in the speech are not bound by any simple form of coherence.

Data Volume

The base of machines capable of handling the bandwidth required to sample, digitize, and reconstitute a high-fidelity sensory experience is increasing. The bandwidth required to satisfy the needs of the visual and auditory senses is approximated by the bandwidth requirements of high-definition television (HDTV) and digital audio compact discs (CDs). Less prominent, but also progressing, are efforts to manage the output bandwidth requirements of the user which include spoken utterances, and fine and gross motor actions. It is valuable to imagine some practical ceiling on the bandwidth requirements of such a system.

Auditory and oral bandwidth requirements might be at the current Audio CD standard, i.e. 0.2 MB/sec.[6] Stereoscopic high-resolution television might be used as the basis for video bandwidth requirements yielding a requirement of 0.4GB/sec.[7] It is hard to imagine input bandwidths that would compete with these video and audio bandwidth requirements. Similarly, it is hard to imagine that some significant compression could not be achieved for the stereoscopic imaging. All of this suggests an ultimate bandwidth requirement in the 0.01GB to 0.5GB range.[8]

Compared to these, it is possible to imagine "information" sources as somewhat more limited. It is well known that the text of a speech requires far less bandwidth than the spoken speech. However, let us consider satellite imaging data. The data from a single pass of a spy satellite over a missile range in 15 minutes can produce more information than can be managed by 100 analysts over a week's period. There are a series of applications of information technology to virtual reality which must manage very large amounts of information or raw data. A well-studied example is the display of tactical, operational, and strategic data to fighter pilots. The idea here is to restructure all the data of possible interest to the pilot and present it all simultaneously, or at least on demand in such a way that the disparate information forms and sources seem coherent. In operating rooms, it is now possible to sample the majority of the analog measurements of a patient's status as well as input measurements of drugs or gases being administered to the patient during surgery. How can this deluge of data be presented to the surgeon to avoid interfering with the procedure, and simultaneously provide an early warning system for trouble? Using virtual realities for information management need not be restricted to rarefied environments. Another example is the automobile driver who has access to every potentially important bit of information about driving. Diagnostics on all fluid levels, immediate road conditions, vectors of other drivers, traffic patterns en route, can be detected and made available to the driver to avoid accidents due to drunk driving, brake failure, the unavailability of windshield washer fluid or poor/hazardous road conditions. The potential bandwidth to be managed in these kinds of situations far exceeds the bandwidth for stereo images and sounds presented in more mundane depictions of reality as we know it. This concern makes Lewis's (1989) work on metaphoric visualization of crucial importance.

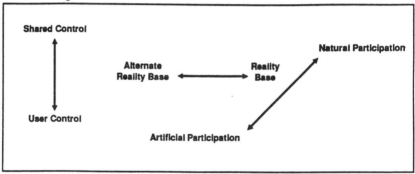

Figure 1. Dimensions of Virtual Reality Systems

The Type of Data or Information

The basis of the constructed reality is important to consider. One prominent basis, and the most researched at this point, is the physical universe. The universe of ideas represents another candidate for visualization. A hundred thousand data inputs forming the picture of a dog are quickly resolved to a small number of pulses by the human brain, which identifies the dog as "Lassie." On the other hand, a relatively simple data input such as the word "Lassie" might conjure memories of significant bandwidth in the listener, such as the recall of all the movie and television characters or the script of some particular episode, or even one's own dogs. Language is an abstraction of reality with words and symbols representing various information loadings to

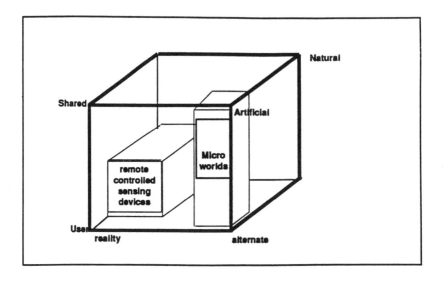

Figure 2. Categorization of Virtual Reality Systems

the receiver. Thus, the equation $e=mc^2$ has different information loadings for a physicist and a high school physics student.

A virtual reality could be developed that allows a researcher to walk through a physical library. That would be a rather simple task when compared to creating a virtual reality allowing the same researcher to walk through the same library space to see some aspect of the ideas represented by book titles rather than just seeing book spines. Consider a system that allows the user to visualize the potential importance of the volumes to a particular research problem. Imagine walking into a virtual library with a query and having all irrelevant data sources appear black, all contrary evidence appear in shades from maroon to bright red, all supporting ideas represented in shades from midnight blue to blue-white, while related concepts could be depicted in shades of green and yellow. As the researcher continues and the research problem is modified, the shades and colors of the entire collection of ideas are modified to reflect the support and contradiction of the new theories. While the communications and processing bandwidth required to provide the sensory stimulation are the same as described earlier (0.1-0.5GB), the density of the data and information underlying the image requires a potentially much greater bandwidth. Let us consider a library of 100,000 (10^5) volumes. An average volume might present a data store of 10MB or 10^6 bytes.[9] Thus, the library represents a data store of 10^{11} bytes or 100GB. This information must be continually researched, culled, organized, filtered, and represented to the user as the search progresses and the query posed by the user is modified.

While this particular virtual reality has not yet been proposed, to the best of my knowledge, a number of authors conducting research on hypertext browsers have experimented with methods for depicting large idea spaces; Conklin and Begemen (1987), Crouch, Crouch, and Andreas (1989), and Lesk (1989). What is important is rather than endeavoring to depict the idea space in concrete terms—the usual effort in metaphoric visualization—the effort would be to develop some quasi-mental visualization of the search process. The example above suggests that the researcher sees supporting and contradicting evidence and ideas in hot and cold colors. This example could be taken further to associate names in different sizes floating near the bright splotches of color as a mechanism for depicting authors who have written major pieces or are frequently referenced in works related to the query. Again, the effort is to suggest visual metaphors for mental models of how the idea space is organized. The important point here is that information spaces can be much denser data sources than visual spaces.

Relationships among the Data/Information Elements

In visualizing a tree, the relation between two leaves is physically depicted by their spatial proximity, while the relation between two auditory signals is depicted by their temporal proximity. Visually, one data source is connected to those that are contiguous in the x, y, and z dimensions. Auditorially, one data source may be connected to others in the temporal, frequency, and amplitude dimensions. How do we depict the relationship of two ideas, or bits of information?

This is a major problem under study by a number of researchers working on hypertext and hypermedia. The dominant model is based upon the computer model of nodes and links, with links as a binary reality. While more recent studies have begun to expand our conception of links (DeRose, 1989; Evenson, Rheinfrank, and Wulff,1989), most distinctions remain more qualitative rather than quantitative.

Consider again the previous example—a user searching an information space. Add to the visual rainbow of ideas some mechanism for connecting the ideas. In contrast to the binary link model, consider a model that borrows from the work of connectionists the notion of weighted links. The ideological library might show not only the color splotches described in the previous section but connections between and among the ideas represented in the library depicted by links showing the nature and strength of the connections between various ideas. Solid, thick links would show important connections and thin ephemeral links would show incidental connections. Links would shrink and grow in solidity and diameter as the researcher develops the query and moves through the space. Focusing techniques would prevent the web from becoming a nightmare of ubiquitous connections. Regardless of the form, new techniques will be required to show the kinds of connections that can exist in information and data generally not required for sensory signals.

Conclusion

Virtual realities suggest a new era in human computer interface design. The dominant characteristic of these efforts is the development of systems that allow users to more fully experience the totality of the simulated environment. The physical world simulation presents real and difficult research problems to be studied and resolved. The world of ideas presents additional difficulties and opportunities for the researcher interested in virtual realities. Central aspects of these problems include data density, aggregation of data, and data interconnectedness.

If virtual realities are to be used in the process of informating, several questions will have to be addressed:

1. How do humans process ideas? How are they visualized, if at all, internally? What visual metaphors are used, and how common are they?
2. What models explain visualization and manipulation of ideas?
3. What is the most appropriate interface for addressing a given data or information related problem? What levels of interface naturalness, reality modeling, and system/user control are required?
4. How can large data sources be filtered and managed?
5. How can the interconnectedness of ideas be visualized?

Notes

1. The Palo Alto Research Center of the Xerox Corporation.
2. The term *intelligence* is used here most casually. The issue of true machine intelligence is not addressed. Rather, the user's perception of such is accepted as enough to merit characterization of the interface as being intelligent. A classic example of such a system is one called Eliza.

3. The suggestion that the STAR and successor environments are crude is only in the context of virtual reality systems. The STAR still remains one of the most sophisticated metaphoric direct manipulations systems, a significant tribute given its age.

4. Organized pattern of signals.

5. *Information* is variously defined by scholars in the field. This chapter's working definition of information is data which reduces entropy for a given individual. That is to say, data which changes the state of awareness of an individual so as to reduce uncertainty. The data "It is raining outside" is information to an individual who was unaware of the state of the weather and is not information to the individual who was aware of the state of the weather.

6. Current standards for digital audio compact disc are 44,056 samples per second with the range per sample captured as a sixteen bit value (0 to 2^{16} -1). This requires a channel capacity of 0.1MB per channel, or a total of 0.2MB/sec. to handle both auditory output and speech input.

7. There are competing standards for HDTV so no standard figure can be achieved. For purposes of illustration, a 1,000 line screen with a 1 to 1 aspect ratio yields 1,000,000 pixels per screen. Pixel values are determined by a 24-bit value, 8-bits each for red, green, and blue, and it is assumed that a refresh rate of 60 cycles per second is adopted. This calculation yields 180MB per channel or 360MB for digital stereo HDTV. The figure is rounded up to 0.4GB to allow for the somewhat higher line resolution suggested in several standards.

8. It is important to note that these estimates do not necessarily reflect end point to end point bandwidth requirements, particularly for alternate realities where relatively small (less than 0.01MB) transmissions would cause local processing and display of significant amounts of data for a visual display. For example, Media Lab experiments with local storage of images of a face and the 16 possible lip configurations make it possible to present a convincing image of a speaker with a transmission of less than 40 bytes per second, versus the 180,000,000 bytes per second required for live HDTV image. (Brand, pp.146-147)

9. Consider an average book of 200 pages, with an average of 800 six-letter words per page and an equivalent amount of font and display information. This yields about 10KB/page or 2MB/book. If the book has 7 1MB images and 50 20KB graphics, the total storage requirement for the book will be 10MB.

References

Brand, S., *The Media Lab: Inventing the Future at M.I.T.* New York: Viking, 1987.

Cattaneo, G., Guercio, A., Levialdi, S. and Tortora, G., "IconLisp: An Example of a Visual Programming Language," *Proceedings of the 1986 IEEE Computer Society Workshop on Visual Languages.* June 25–27, 1986, Dallas, Texas, pp. 22–25.

Chang, S.-K., Tauber, M.J., Yu, B., and Yu, J.-S., "A Visual Language Compiler," *IEEE Transactions of Software Engineering.* Vol.15, No. 5, May 1989, pp. 506–525.

Chang, S.-K., "Visual Reasoning for Information Retrieval from Very Large Databases" *Proceedings of the 1989 IEEE Workshop on Visual Languages.* October 4–6 1989, Rome, Italy, pp. 1–6.

Conklin, J. and Begemen, M.L. "IBIS: A Hypertext Tool for Team Design Deliberation," *Hypertext '87 Proceedings.* November 13–15, 1987, Chapel Hill, North Carolina, pp. 247–252.

Crouch, D.B., Crouch, C.J., and Andreas, G., "The Use of Cluster Hierarchies in Hypertext Information Retrieval," *Hypertext '89 Proceedings.* November 5–8, 1989, Pittsburgh, Pennsylvania, pp. 225–237.

Crouch, D.B., "A Pictorial Representation of Data in an Information Retrieval Environment," *1987 Workshop on Visual Languages.* August 19–21, 1987, Tryck-Center, Linkoping, Sweden: pp. 177–187.

DeFanti, T.A., Brown, M.D., and McCormick, B.H., "Visualization: Expanding Scientific and Engineering Research Opportunities," *Computer.* Vol. 22, No. 6, August 1989, pp. 12–26.

DeRose, S.J., "Expanding the Notion of Links," *Hypertext '89 Proceedings.* November 5–8, 1989, Pittsburgh, Pennsylvania, pp. 249–258.

Elmer-Dewitt, P., "Through the 3-D Looking Glass," *Time.* Vol. 133, No. 18, May 1, 1989, pp. 65–66.

Evenson, S., Rheinfrank, J. and Wulff, W., "Toward a Design Language for Representing Hypermedia Cues," *Hypertext '89 Proceedings.* November 5–8, 1989, Pittsburgh, Pennsylvania, pp. 83–92.

Farmer, F.R., "Cyberspace: Getting There From Here," *Journal of Computer Game Design.* October 1988.

Glinert, E.P., "Toward 'Second Generation' Interactive, Graphical Programming Environments," *Proceedings of the 1986 IEEE Computer Society Workshop on Visual Languages.* June 25–27, 1986, Dallas, Texas, pp. 61–70.

Korfhage, R.K., "Browser—A Concept for Visual Navigation of a Database," *Proceedings of the 1986 IEEE Computer Society Workshop on Visual Languages.* June 25–27, 1986, Dallas, Texas, pp. 143–148.

Lesk, M., "What to Do When There Is Too Much Information," *Hypertext '89 Proceedings*. November 5–8, 1989, Pittsburgh, Pennsylvania, pp. 305–318.

Lewis, M.L., "Metaphor in Visualization," Working Paper, Department of Information Science, University of Pittsburgh, Pennsylvania, 1989.

McCormick, B.H. et al (ed.), "Visualization in Scientific Computing," *Computer Graphics*. Vol. 21, No. 6, November 1987.

Rohr, G., "Understanding Visual Symbols," *Proceedings of the 1984 IEEE Computer Society Workshop on Visual Languages*. December 6–8, 1984, Hiroshima, Japan, pp. 184–191.

Selker, T. and Koved, L. "Elements of Visual Language," *Proceedings of the 1988 IEEE Computer Society Workshop on Visual Languages*. October 10–12, 1988, Pittsburgh, Pennsylvania, pp. 38–44.

Smith, D., Irby, C., Kimball, R., and Verplank, B. "Designing the Star User Interface," *Byte*, April 1982, pp. 242–282.

Smith, R.B., "The Alternate Reality Kit: An Animated Environment for Creating Interactive Simulations" *Proceedings of the 1986 IEEE Computer Society Workshop on Visual Languages*. June 25–27, 1986, Dallas, Texas, pp. 99–106.

Stefik, M. et al, "Beyond the Chalkboard: Computer Support for Collaboration and Problem Solving in Meetings," *Communications of the ACM*, Vol. 30, No. 1, January 1987, pp. 32–37.

Zuboff, S., *In the Age of the Smart Machine: The Future of Work and Power*. New York: Basic Books Inc., 1984.

Artificial Reality: Past and Future

Myron W. Krueger

As a graduate student at the University of Wisconsin in the late 1960s, I considered the encounter between human and machine as the central drama of our time. The connection between them was a permanent part of the human condition, as fundamental as particle physics and deserving of comparable research efforts. It seemed that there were two ingredients: the computer and the person. One was evolving faster than any technology in history; the other was not evolving at all. Whereas the user interface had always been a veneer applied to the computer to make it slightly easier to use, it seemed obvious that the ultimate interface would be to the human body and human senses.

Several years earlier (in the early 1960s), a similar thought process had led Ivan Sutherland (University of Utah) to identify the next logical step in the development of computer graphics. He implemented a head-mounted display that allowed a person to look around in a graphic room by simply turning their head. Two small CRTs driven by vector graphics generators provided the appropriate stereo view for each eye. In the early 1970s, Fred Brooks (University of North Carolina) created a system that allowed a person to handle graphic objects by using a mechanical manipulator. When the user moved the physical manipulator, a graphic manipulator moved accordingly. If a graphic block was picked up, the user felt its weight and its resistance to their fingers closing around it.

Beginning in 1969, I created a series of interactive environments that emphasized unencumbered, full-body, multi-sensory participation in computer events. In one demonstration, a sensory floor detected participants' movements around a room. A symbol representing them moved through a projected graphic maze that changed in playful ways if participants tried to cheat. In another demonstration, participants could use the image of a finger to draw on the projection screen. In yet another, participants' views of a projected three-dimensional room changed appropriately as they moved around the physical space.

It was impressive to observe how technologically naive people naturally accepted these projected experiences as reality. They expected their bodies to influence graphic objects and were delighted when they did. They regarded their electronic image as an extension of themselves. What happened to their image also happened to them; they felt what touched their image. If I superimposed my image on their image, personal distance was observed; people avoided touching, or they deliberately touched in a playful way.

The Beginnings of Videoplace

These observations led me to create the Videoplace, a graphic world that people could enter from different places to interact with each other and with graphic creatures.* Since participants' live video images can be manipulated (moved, scaled, rotated) in real time, the world created was not bound by the laws of physics. In fact, the result was an artificial reality in which the laws of cause and effect are created and can be changed from moment to moment. Indeed, I coined the term 'artificial reality' to describe the type of experience that could be created with Videoplace or with the technology invented by Ivan Sutherland.

In February 1972, the first draft of a manuscript that became my dissertation in 1974 was completed, and finally published as *Artificial Reality* (Addison-Wesley, 1983); an updated version will appear this summer (1990). *Artificial Reality* describes Videoplace as well as highly portable data goggles, a data glove and a data suit with force feedback.

The day after my final oral examination in July 1974, I went to Washington, D.C. to propose Videoplace as the theme of the Bicentennial, a reprise of a Centennial exhibit that had featured the telephone. Environments were planned for both the East and West coasts of the United States as well as in Europe and Japan. Every government agency and a number of large corporations were approached with the expectation that these ideas would be enthusiastically greeted. To my shock, DARPA (Defense Advanced Research Projects Agency) said that human-machine interaction had been done. NSF (National Science Foundation) said, "That sounds like engineering!" NASA stated that

---

*Videoplace is an installation at the Connecticut Museum of Natural History in Storrs, CT. Videoplace visitors in separate rooms can fingerpaint together, perform free-fall gymnastics, tickle each other, and experience additional interactive events. The computer combines and alters input from separate cameras trained on each person, who responds in turn to the computer's output, playing games in the world created by Videoplace software.

there was a satellite available provided I could get it launched. In fact, the only person who said, "Let's do it" was from the Japanese embassy.

When contacted to write this chapter, I was asked to comment on why artificial realities had taken so long to take hold. The history of these ideas provides an interesting case study in the process of innovation. The ingredients were available in the early 1970s. So, what happened?

Research and Development

First, it is not uncommon for isolated early research to precede more broad-based research and practical application by many years. Expert systems, neural nets, and robotics are all technologies that were abandoned by the research community after early successes. Researchers operate under a set of constraints that are very difficult to resist. In order to survive, they must publish in journals but there are few journals for new technologies, only for established ones. Similarly, if there is no funding, there is no way to perform the research. In addition, after the initial feasibility has been demonstrated, follow up attempts are perceived as redundant. A decade or so later, when the practical application of a technology is unavoidable, the same topic can suddenly support hundreds of papers.

There were also a number of profoundly American prejudices operating. First, researchers are supposed to work with pure "science." Therefore, the legitimate role of engineering and invention are denied. Second, research is directed at national needs as perceived by government agencies and big companies. While DARPA funded a few human interface projects at Massachusetts Institute of Technology (M.I.T.) and the U.S. Air Force developed the heads-up display, there was not a broadly based research interest in the human interface. There was also timidity caused by Senator William Proxmire's ridicule for any projects he did not understand. His influence caused a tremendous distortion of the research process and cost the country more than all his collective golden fleece victims. Finally, because of how research is funded, we are too often blind to technologies that can be used by individuals rather than organizations. In 1983, I wrote, "With the recent and *probably temporary exception* of video games, we buy almost all of our entertainment technology from other countries." The experience of seeing American inventions, such as the transistor radio and the VCR, produced abroad is repeated over and over. Even when we are first to commercialize a technology, we are not entirely comfortable in these markets. The collapse of the video games market was greeted with a sigh of relief by the American business community. Similarly, home computers were abandoned without a fight. American technology is for business and government; consumers must look elsewhere.

Geography was another factor. Utah, North Carolina and Wisconsin are not even on the media map of American technology. The importance of this technology coming from NASA cannot be overestimated. Innovation is supposed to come through certain channels, meaning NASA, M.I.T., CMU and Silicon Valley. If it has other origins, it may flounder for years before given any attention.

A Changing Point of View

Given that artificial realities were outside the official research goals of the 1970s, what changed? Interactive computing has become the norm. Until recently, the personal computer market has been growing far faster than the "old" mainframe market. Computer-human interaction is now officially a branch of Computer Science, and SIGCHI (Special Interest Group for Computer Human Interaction) is the fastest growing part of the ACM (Association for Computing Machinery). These developments provide an audience for the results but do not explain why specific research was undertaken. There was one enabling technology and one force that explains why it is now receiving so much attention.

The tiny flat panel displays that were being used for hand-held portable televisions were suitable for 3-D goggles. Michael McGreevy at NASA apparently noticed the same thing in 1984 when he developed the data goggles allowing a participant to look around a graphic world. It was significant not because any new ideas were produced, but because it was very inexpensive. The data goggles were possible because of a Japanese consumer product! (In keeping with a new trend, American scientists now take apart Japanese toys to create new research instruments.)

The original development of NASA's technology happened during the years 1984 to 1985. Since then, there have not been any significant breakthroughs. It is naive to think that we are seeing a spontaneous ground swell of interest in new ideas. NASA appears to be promoting artificial realities more than the space program. In 1985, when I first met Jaron Lanier, the chairman of VPL, he could not get the Data Glove manufactured because the video game market was dead. We owe a debt to Nintendo for resurrecting the business in which we participated reluctantly.

In addition, the entry of a second company, Autodesk, creates the appearance of an industry. Obviously, it is natural for these companies to promote their products. This is made easier because they are now working with high-quality color graphics. While these high-resolution images cannot be displayed on the data goggles, they are perfect for magazines and video coverage.

Public Awareness and Its Results

Now that there are products based on this technology, artificial reality has become a newsworthy story. In particular, the headline "What is Artificial Reality?" on the front page of the *New York Times* (April 10, 1989) was a turning point. Once this subject was thus ratified, people began to feel comfortable showing their interest, or are now being motivated to learn more.

Absent from this discussion is any positive role for the innovation establishment. When McGreevy began his work in the mid 1980s, neither NASA, NSF nor DARPA would entertain proposals on this topic. NASA itself was as much a victim as a hero of the tale. The only academic work at the time was my own at the University of Connecticut (Storrs, CT). There was no apparent interest on the part of intellectuals, scientists or corporations. In fact, there was none until 1985, when operational Videoplace and NASA technologies were revealed.

Now that toys using this technology are being manufactured, there is a mass movement in the intellectual and research communities; scientific conferences are being scheduled, academic programs are forming and books are being published. Journals and dissertations will, no doubt, follow. It is important to note the role of invention in engineering areas. Until a technology exists, there is a considerable unwillingness to speculate, theorize, fund or publish. What has been done so far is invention; research has not yet begun.

Applications for the Consumer

The Artificial Reality Corporation has two operational prototype technologies. One prototype is encumbering and three-dimensional, and the other unencumbering and temporarily two- dimensional. The question for the moment is whether people will be willing to wear goggles and gloves to go about their daily business. The experience of 3-D movies suggests that there will be resistance. Immediate candidates for goggles and gloves are people who have to suit up to go to work already, such as pilots and astronauts. Children will cheerfully don paraphernalia that creates more realistic video games. Broader application may also be inhibited by the low-resolution of the liquid crystal displays.

Videoplace is quite different because it is easy to enter. Your face need not be obscured to those around you or to those in Videoplace. Videodesk is a variation on this technology in which hands rest on your desk and appear on the computer screen. They can be used to control many existing applications, and can appear on a colleague's computer screen a thousand miles away. An individual can use his or her hands to help talk about the information on the screen as if several individuals were together talking about a piece of paper.

A synthesis of the two technologies is inevitable. *Artificial Reality* suggests the possibility of see-through glasses and even contact lenses. With such small glasses, video cameras can see your face and provide a three-dimensional alter ego. In fact, the graphic reality and the real one can be merged so that teleparticipants can appear to be sitting on real chairs around you.

There will also be a temporary step backward in the technology. The current VPL demonstration of NASA's technology costs approximately $300,000 per person. Looking back ten years ago, the cost of computer graphics has declined dramatically in comparison, but not enough to make artificial realities an everyday experience in the near future. On the other hand, line graphics, stereo videodisc images, and a hundred other short cuts can be taken to produce low-cost systems until true three-dimensional graphics are affordable. Multimedia and artificial realities will soon merge.

Future Developments

Looking forward, there is a wonderful opportunity for exploratory research; that is, researching ourselves. What is reality to us? What can we adapt to? Perception will be studied as part of active behavior rather than as a separate sedentary behavior. Communication will be studied since it is possible to capture everything that passes between two people in ways never before possible.

Artificial reality is a new concept which can be applied to almost every human activity. For example, it is a cliche that experience is the best teacher. But, what if concise educational experiences could be composed? In 1976, I suggested that children act as if scientists landing on an alien planet, charged with discovering the local physics and the behavior of the local fauna. This was to be a deliberately nontraditional world in which adults would be at a disadvantage. In this world children would learn the process of being a scientist rather than the vocabulary and "puzzle-solving" of traditional science courses.

Artificial realities are part of ongoing trends. Most obvious is the trend from interaction to participation in computer events and active versus passive art forms. It is also part of the increasing significance of artificial experiences over real ones. Businessmen talk about "doing it right the first time." However, this fantasy is possible not because fewer mistakes are being made, but because the mistakes are being made in simulated environments.

There is also a trend from the conceptual to the perceptual, a renewed respect for innate, intuitive, real world intelligence over acquired, abstract, symbolic intelligence. More and more, people will seek ways to visualize what used to be represented mathematically because perceptual intelligence is the result of millions of years of evolution, whereas abstract symbol manipulation skills are a much more recent and less mature development.

Most importantly, artificial realities are a medium of expression and experience, as well as a new way for people to interact with each other. These uses of artificial reality will be as economically important as the "practical" applications (entertainment is the United States' number two export). Increasingly, people are products of artificial experience. Vicarious experience through theater, novels, movies and television represents a significant fraction of our lives. The addition of a radically new form of physically involving, interacterive experience is a major cultural event which may shape our consciousness as much as what has come before.

The Metaphysics of Virtual Reality

Michael Heim

The commission money was good and the artist arrived on time. One of the executives from corporate design was there to meet her at the door. After touring the facilities, the artist was left alone to begin painting. Each day the mural materialized a bit more, section by section, spreading a ribbon of color across the large gray wall at the end of the lobby. First a green patch of forest glade appeared, two blossoming plum trees, three sky-blue vistas, and a Cheshire cat on a branch. Finally the day came when the tarp would fall. Employees gathered around plastic cups and croissants. When the speeches were over, the room grew hushed for the unveiling. The crowd gasped. The wall came alive with paradise, an intricate world of multicolored shapes. Several employees lingered to chat with the artist. Once the congratulations died down, the artist strolled to the center of the mural, stopping where the garden path leads into the forest, and, with face to the crowd, she smiled, bowed, and turned her back. Walking into the green leaves, she was never seen again.

This ancient story, adapted from Taoist legend, anticipates the metaphysics of virtual reality. On one level, the story praises the power of artistic illusion. On a deeper level, it suggests the need we have to create realities within realities, to suspend belief in one set of involvements in order to entertain another. The story depicts our ability to enter symbolic space where we move about in alternate worlds. Whether we read a short story, watch a film or contemplate a painting, we enjoy being hijacked to another plane of being. Our capacity to immerse ourselves in a symbolic element has developed to where we hardly even notice the disappearing act. We slip off into symbolic existence at the drop of "Once upon a time" or "Given any variable X."

From Naive Realism to Irrealism

Are not all worlds symbolic? Including the one we naively refer to as the real world which we read off with our physical senses? Philosophers as recent as Nelson Goodman and Richard Rorty have considered all

27

worlds—not just the world of story-telling and film-making—to be contingent symbolic constructs. Science, religion, and art provide different versions which are made, tested, and known in diverse ways, each with its own rightness and function. Each world is made from the previous world(s), and each process of worldmaking proceeds by composing or decomposing older materials, by identifying repetitions and evolving new patterns, by deleting and supplementing, by organizing and ordering aspects of the world(s) already there. One well-worn way to point out this diversity is to compare the weather vocabulary of Eskimos with that of the surf riders in Southern California.

When did the universe break into a plurality? Since Immanuel Kant, philosophy has moved gradually from the unique reality of a single fixed world to a diversity of worlds. Kant eliminated the notion of a pre-given world by locating orderly patterns not in the found world but in the architecture of the human mind. The categories of the understanding (causality and substance) along with the forms of intuition (space and time) mold the chaotic givens of perception, forging an intelligible, communicable structure of experience. Still, Kant postulated a monistic ideal of unity to regulate our construction of the world. The world we make, he thought, drives toward a single shared unity. In this way, Kant protected the Newtonian science of his era by basing knowledge on the supposedly absolute forms lodged in human reasoning. After Kant, philosophers whittled away at the monistic unity until quantum theory in the twentieth century withdrew support for the kind of coherence Kant thought essential to science. Now, with science itself open to diversity and indeterminateness, many philosophers welcome the world as a plurality. In our day, Nelson Goodman, for instance, says: "Our passion for *one* world is satisfied, at different times and for different purposes, in *many* different ways. Not only motion, derivation, weighting, order, but even reality is relative" (p. 20). Goodman's *Ways of Worldmaking*, in which he promotes the doctrine of irrealism, seems a proper primer for the architects of virtual reality.

Realism and Irrealism—
Both Unrealistic

Yet irrealism may be short-sighted. We may need to hang on to a notion of the real world, if not out of abstract conviction then at least out of the need for occasional reality checks against our virtual reality systems. An unrestrained proliferation of worlds cries out for sanity, for connection with reality, for metaphysical grounding. Kant dismissed metaphysical theories as idle sophistries and intellectual games played by charlatans. Philosophers in the twentieth century, from Wittgenstein and Heidegger to Carnap and Ayer, followed Kant in side-stepping metaphysics, believing it to be an ungrounded spin of the linguistic wheels, or a chase after vague vapor trails, or simply a logical mistake. For this line of thinking, reality has lost its meaning as a serious term. The coming VR engines may force a change in that general line of thought and shed new light on classical metaphysics. The next century may have to dig again in a very ancient field of metaphysics excavated by the engines of computer-simulated virtual reality, the metaphysical machine par excellence. Conversely, virtual realities may be all the richer for preserving some relationship to a real world without, however, becoming boring or mundane.

The terms "real" and "virtual" need sorting out before we relate them to each other. I find the contemporary usage of the term, as well as its distant ancestor, enlightening.

The Vocabulary of Virtuality

In contemporary usage, the virtual in "virtual reality" comes from software engineering. Computer scientists use "virtual memory" to mean computer RAM set aside in such a way that the computer operates as if memory exists beyond the actual hardware limits. The term virtual has come to connote any sort of computer phenomenon, from virtual mail to virtual work groups on computer networks, to virtual libraries and even virtual universities. In each case, the adjective refers to a reality that is not a formal, bona fide reality. When we call cyberspace a virtual space, we mean a not-quite-actual space, something existing in contrast to the real hardware space but operative as if it were real space. Cyberspace seems to take place within the framework of real space.

The virtual in "virtual reality" goes back to a linguistic distinction formulated in medieval Europe. The medieval logician Duns Scotus (died 1308) gave the term its traditional connotations. His Latin *virtualiter* served as the centerpiece of his theory of reality. The Doctor of Subtlety maintained that the concept of a thing contains empirical attributes not in a formal way (as if the thing were knowable apart from empirical observations) but *virtualiter* or virtually. Though we may have to dig into our experiences to unveil the qualities of a thing, Scotus held, the real thing already contains its manifold empirical qualities in a single unity, but it contains them virtually—otherwise they would not stick as qualities of that thing. Scotus used the term virtual to bridge the gap between formally unified reality (as defined by our conceptual expectations) and our messily diverse experiences. Similarly, we nowadays use the term virtual to breach the gap between a given environment and a further level of man-made accretions. Virtual space—as opposed to natural bodily space—contains the informational equivalent of things. Virtual space makes us feel as if we were dealing directly with physical or natural realities. As if . . .

Our as-if stops short of Scotus' term, for he could assume, with all classical metaphysicians, that our concepts fit squarely with the eternally fixed essences of things. Scotus could assign a merely virtual reality to some aspects of experience because he believed his primary experience already exhibited "real reality," to use Plato's strange phrase. Classical and medieval philosophy equated reality with the permanent features of experience, and this naive realism anchored human beings in the world. The medievals believed the anchor held with all the weight of an all-powerful, unchanging God.

We cannot locate the anchor for our reality check outside this fluctuating, changing world. No universal divinity insures an invariant stability for things. But we need some sense of metaphysical anchoring, I think, to enhance virtual worlds. A virtual world can be virtual only as long as we can contrast it with the real (anchored) world. Virtual worlds can then maintain an aura of imaginary reality, a multiplicity that is playful rather than maddening.

A virtual world needs to be not-quite-real or it will lessen the pull on imagination. Something-less-than real evokes our power of imaging and visualization. Recall the legend of the vanishing artist. The magic within the story comes from the crossover of three-dimensional to two-dimensional frameworks. On another level, the magic of the story comes from our ability to cross over from the words of the narration to an inner vision of the sequence of virtual events (which occurs in us as we walk through the wall of words on the page). The story relates a legend about the power of symbols while at the same time exhibiting that power. Imagination allows us to take what we read or hear and reconstitute the symbolic components into a mental vision. The vision transcends the limits of our bodily reality, so that, from the viewpoint of bodily existence, imagination is an escape—even though imagination often introduces new factors into our lives which sometimes cause us to alter our actual circumstances.

For the most part, imagination receives in order to create. We take the words of a story or the flickering photos of a film and reconstitute their contents, customizing the narrative details to our own understanding. Especially when using a single sense, like hearing or touch, we are active in receiving information. All the other senses subconsciously join to reconstitute the content. But imagination always leaves behind the limits of our physical existence, and for this reason it is "only" imagination. Because it leaves the real world behind, imagination is not reality. When the artist takes her body with her through the mural painting, it is our imagination (through the story) that completes her work of art.

The Virtues of Cyberspace

Cyberspace too evokes our imagination. Cyberspace is the broad electronic net in which virtual realities are spun. Virtual reality is only one type of phenomenon within electronic space. Cyberspace, as a general medium, invites participation. In the framework of the everyday world, cyberspace is the set of orientation points by which we find our way around a bewildering amount of data. Working on a mainframe computer, like the Cyber 960 or the VAX 6320, we must learn to sketch a mental map for navigating the system. Without a subconsciously familiar map, we soon lose our way in the information wilderness. Using a desktop or portable computer requires a similar internal depiction of how hardware, CRT, keyboard, and disk drives connect, even if the picture is mythical or anthropomorphic—just as long as it works. Magnetic storage offers no three-dimensional cues for physical bodies, so we must develop our own internally imaged sense of the data topology. This inner map we make for ourselves, plus the layout of the software, is cyberspace.

The familiar mental map compares to the full-featured virtual reality like radio to television, or like television to three-dimensional bodily experience. In its simplest form, cyberspace activates the user's creative imagination. As it becomes more elaborate, cyberspace develops real-world simulations and then virtual realities. William Gibson's cyberspace presents the data of the international business community as a three-dimensional videogame. Gibson's users get involved through a computer console connected by electrodes feeding directly into the brain. The user's body stays behind to punch the deck and give the coordinates, while the user's mind roams the computer matrix. The user feels the body to be "meat" or a chiefly passive material component of cyberspace while the online mind lives blissfully on its own. His novel *Neuromancer* describes the passivity of cyberspace as "a consensual hallucination... A graphic representation of data abstracted from the banks of every computer in the human system. Unthinkable complexity." On the active side, the user pursues "the lines of light ranged in the nonspace of the mind."

Virtual Realities without Ontological Security

The problem is not with cyberspace but with virtual reality. I do not have to imagine myself bodily entering into a virtual world. The computer's VR will soon allow me to take my body along with me, either with a sensorium interface or with a third-person iconic representation. The degree of realism is in principle unlimited. This very realism may turn into irrealism where virtual worlds are indistinguishable from real worlds, where virtual reality gets bland and mundane, where users undergo predominantly passive experiences akin to drug-induced hallucinations. If Schopenhauer is right when he says that we are incorrigibly metaphysical animals, then this irrealism violates something we need and puts a possible limit on virtual reality construction.

How may we preserve the contrast between virtual and real worlds? How can virtual realities preserve a built-in contrast to real or anchored reality so we will enjoy a metaphysical pull to create and actively use our imaginations in cyberspace? What anchor can serve to keep virtual worlds virtual?

This is no place to launch a full-scale "battle of the Titans," as Plato described metaphysics. But I want to suggest some existential aspects of the real world which provide clues for preventing a virtual world from flattening out into a literal *déja vu*. These existential features, evolving from twentieth-century philosophy, stand open to revision. Virtual worlds evoke imagination only if they do not simply reproduce the existential features of reality but transform them beyond immediate recognition. The existential features of the real world I refer to include: mortality/natality, carryover between past and future, and care.

The Three Hooks on the Reality Anchor

The real world, conceived existentially, functions with built-in constraints. These constraints provide parameters for human meaning. One constraint, our inevitable mortality, marks human existence as finite. Because of a limited life span, we demarcate our lives into periods of passage as well as into the schedules and deadlines that order our work flow. We are born at a definite time (natality) and grow up within distinct interactions (family kinships). These limits impose existential parameters on reality, providing us with a sense of rootedness in the earth (a finite planet with fragile ecosystems). Mortality/natality belongs to the reality anchor. Another reality constraint is temporality, the built-in carryover of events from the past into the future, our memory or history. We can erase nothing in principle from what happens in a lifetime. What the

German language calls *Einmaligkeit* or "once-and-always-ness" endows actions with uniqueness and irretrievability. The carryover feature distinguishes reality from any passing entertainment or momentary hallucination. Finally, because of the temporariness of biological life forms, a sense of fragility or precariousness pervades our real world, frequently making suffering a default value. The possibility of physical injury in the real world anchors us in an ultimate seriousness, the poignancy of which lurks behind casual phrases like "Take care." We care because we are fragile and have to be careful. These three features mark human existence and stamp experience with degrees of reality. They anchor us.

Should synthetic worlds then contain no death, no pain, no fretful concerns? To banish finite constraints might disqualify virtuality from having any degree of reality whatsoever. Yet to incorporate constraints fully, as some fiction does, is to produce an empty mirror over and above the real world, a mere reflection of the world in which we are anchored. (I think of Bobby Newmark in *Count Zero,* and the dead boy Wilson carried off Big Playground on a stretcher.) Actual cyberspace should do more; cyberspace should evoke imagination, not repeat the world. Virtual reality could be a place for reflection, but the reflection should make philosophy, not redundancy. "Philosophy," said William James, "is the habit of always seeing an alternative." Cyberspace can contain many alternate worlds, but the alternateness of an alternate world resides in its capacity to evoke in us alternate thoughts and alternate feelings.

Any world needs constraints and finite structure. But which aspects of the real (existential) world can attract our attention and sustain our imagination? Time must be built in, but the way of reckoning time need not duplicate the deadlines of the real world. Time could have the spaciousness of a totally focused project or could be reckoned by rituals of leisure. Danger and caution pervade the real (existential) world, but virtual reality can offer total safety, like the law of sanctuary in religious cultures. Care will always belong to human agents, but, with the help of intelligent software agents, cares will weigh on us more lightly.

The ultimate VR is a philosophical experience, probably an experience of the sublime or awesome. For the sublime, as Kant defined it, is the spine-tingling chill that comes from the realization of how small our finite perceptions are in the face of the infinity of possible, virtual worlds we may settle into and inhabit. The final point of a virtual world is to dissolve the constraints of the anchored world so we can lift anchor—not to drift aimlessly without point, but so we can explore anchorage in ever new places and, perhaps, find our way back to experience the most primitive and powerful alternative embedded in the question posed by Leibniz: "Why is there anything at all rather than nothing?"

References

Gibson, William. *Neuromancer.* New York: Ace Books. 1984.

Gibson, William. *Count Zero.* New York: Ace Books. 1986.

Goodman, Nelson. *Ways of Worldmaking.* Indianapolis: Hackett Publishing, 1978.

Heidegger, Martin. *Basic Writings (Being and Time).* D.F. Krell (Ed. and Transl.). New York: Harper & Row, 1977.

Heim, Michael. "The Erotic Ontology of Cyberspace." In *CYBerspace.* Michael Benedikt (Ed.). Cambridge: MIT Press, 1990.

Heim, Michael. *Electric Language: A Philosophical Study of Word Processing.* New Haven: Yale University Press, 1989, © 1987.

Heim, Michael. "Infomania." In *The State of the Language.* Christopher Ricks and Leonard Michaels (eds.). Berkeley: University of California Press, 1990.

Kant, Immanuel. *Observations on the Feeling of the Beautiful and Sublime.* J.T. Goldthwait (Transl.). Berkeley: University of California Press, 1960.

Rorty, Richard. *Philosophy and the Mirror of Nature.* Princeton, N.J.: Princeton University Press, 1980, © 1979.

The Emerging Technology of Cyberspace

Randal Walser

Cyberspace is a new medium that offers a strong sense of being embodied in a virtual reality (as opposed to film, which can effectively portray a virtual reality but without giving its viewers compelling sense they are actually present within the reality). While cyberspace may be the most important new medium since television, there is nothing radically new in the technology that underlies it. The fundamental components are all readily available off the shelf, from the various makers and suppliers of today's personal computer (PCs) technology. In fact, the essential elements of cyberspace technology have been available since the 1960s. Many cyberspaces have already been created by people who can afford sophisticated simulation systems. Today, three factors are stimulating broad interest in the potential of cyberspace: 1) rapid and continuing performance improvements in personal computers, 2) the availability of relatively low-cost, yet powerful, 3-D rendering engines, and 3) a reconception of the relationship between humans and computers.

Fundamentally, a cyberspace is a type of interactive simulation, called a cybernetic simulation, which includes human beings as necessary components. All interactive simulations can involve humans, but involvement is not the same as inclusion. A cybernetic simulation is a dynamic model of a world filled with objects that exhibit lesser or greater degrees of intelligence. Certain objects, called puppets, are controlled by the actions of humans (patrons) whose movements are monitored by an array of sensors. Generally, a puppet in virtual space moves in direct correspondence with a patron in physical space. The basic job of cyberspace technology, besides simulating a world, is to supply a tight feedback loop between patron and puppet, to give the patron the illusion of being literally embodied by the puppet (i.e., the puppet gives the patron a virtual body, and the patron gives the puppet a personality.)

The relationship between patron and puppet is depicted in Figure 1. The puppet monitors the physical world through an assortment of sensors, and acts on the physical world through various effectors. The sensors include 6-D trackers (devices that monitor a physical object's spatial position and orientation), keyboards, joysticks, steering wheels, speedometers, pressure gauges, mice, and voice recognizers, among many others. The effectors include various graphics and video displays, sound generators, resistance controllers, motion platforms, force feedback devices, and so on.

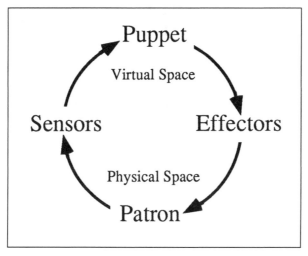

Figure 1. The Cybernetic feedback loop

The paradigm's shift that underlies the emergence of cyberspace is implicit in the use of the terms *sensor* and *effector* in Figure 1. Under the old view, computer systems were designed extrinsically, from the point of view of human "users" who stand outside the system and who use "input devices" to put information in and "output devices" to get information out. A cyberspace system is designed intrinsically, from the point of view of puppets who embody intellects (either human or artificial) within virtual space. Thus the term *sensor*, in Figure 1, refers to a device through which a puppet acquires knowledge of events in physical space. That same device, a keyboard, would have been formerly called an input device. Likewise, a puppet's effectors are output devices in the old way of speaking. Generally, a patron affects virtual space through a puppet's sensors and learns of events in virtual space through a puppet's effectors. That is, a puppet's sensors are a patron's effectors, and a puppet's effectors are a patron's sensors. This can be confusing until you shift your thinking to the intrinsic viewpoint, and realize that discussion is always centered on a point of view from within virtual space (the term *patron*, as another example, is used to suggest an actual visit to a place, such as a museum).

In William Gibson's stories, starting with *Neuromancer*, an instrument called a "deck" is used to "jack" into cyberspace. The instrument that Gibson describes is small enough to fit in a drawer, and directly stimulates the human nervous system. While Gibson's vision is beyond the reach of today's technology, it is nonetheless, today, possible to achieve many of the effects alluded. A number of companies and organizations are actively developing the essential elements of a cyberspace deck (though not everyone has adopted the term *deck*). These groups include NASA, University of North Carolina, University of Washington, Artificial Reality Corp., VPL Research, and Autodesk, along with numerous others who are starting new research and development programs.

At Autodesk, a prototype deck has been under development for about a year. The architecture of the deck is based on the feedback loop illustrated in Figure 1. The central component is an object-oriented simulation system consisting of a small, fast kernel (basically a library of C++ classes), together with a shell that allows programmers to interact directly with data structures and with virtual objects. A "cyberspace," in the implementation, is a cybernetic simulation system consisting of a collection of virtual objects that each get a chance, each simulation cycle, to make whatever contribution they wish to the construction of the next simulation frame (where a "frame" is a descriptive model of the space at one moment in virtual time). This gives great flexibility and power to cyberspace developers, as the system dictates nothing at all about the character of particular spaces. What happens in a space is determined entirely by the behavior of the virtual objects, and that behavior is either programmed by developers or expressed spontaneously by puppets directed by patrons. The kernel contains certain fundamental object classes, like mechanical bodies that can be linked into multibody systems, sensor handlers, and display drivers. Third-party developers can override or specialize the fundamental classes in order to customize their own cyberspace decks.

Besides the simulation system, which runs on an ordinary personal computer (presently only on IBM-PCs or compatibles under DOS), the prototypical deck is made up of six other components: 1) sensors, 2) effectors, 3) a volume of physical space, called a control space, where the movements of patrons are tracked, 4) props, like bicycles, chairs, and railings, that provide physical analogs of virtual objects, 5) an interface to a local area network (presently Ethernet), and 6) an enclosure for all the components (presently an ordinary office space). A typical configuration is illustrated in Figure 2. This configuration, using a treadmill, would enable a patron to walk or run around in a virtual world, point, grasp objects, and issue spoken commands. A similar configuration, using a stationary bicycle (whose virtual analog can fly if it is pedaled fast enough), was implemented and demonstrated at SIGGRAPH '89.

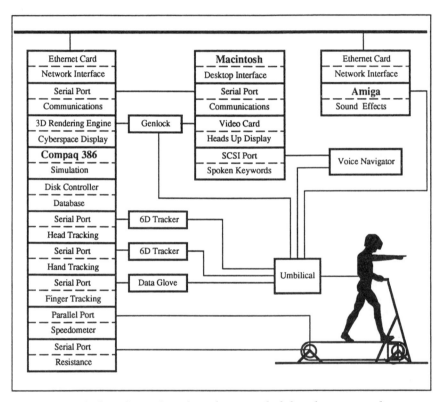

Figure 2. Typical configuration of a cyberspace deck based on personal computer technology. In general a deck is a collection of loosely coupled processors whose activities are synchronized on a single simulation clock. An umbilical is a bundle of cables through which patrons ''jack'' into cyberspace.

Notice that a deck, in Autodesk's approach, is composed of a collection of loosely coupled processors, including whole personal computers. The alternative, usually taken by makers of high-end simulation systems, is to provide all that is necessary in a single box, with all

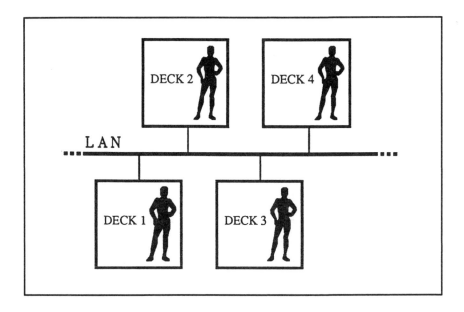

Figure 3. Cyberspace decks linked via a local area network

programs running in a shared memory space. The advantage of the loosely coupled approach is that decks can be built up piecemeal, from low-cost decks, with limited performance capability, consisting of nothing more than an ordinary personal computer, on up to pricey but high performance decks consisting of several personal computers (or a single high performance machine) together with an exotic array of sophisticated sensors and effectors.

At the next level of organization, as shown in Figures 3 and 4, decks are linked into networks that enable more than one person to participate in a space at a time. To date, very little work has been done with multi-person spaces, though VPL Research demonstrated its "Reality Built for Two" system almost a year ago, and is continuing to make rapid improvements. Autodesk has only just begun to develop a multi-person capability, but will soon begin.

Multi-person spaces are especially important, and intriguing, because they promise to be far more lively than spaces in which an individual can interact only with a computer. In a multi-person space there will always be a possibility (at least under Autodesk's approach) that the virtual objects encountered are directed by human intelligence, though they may be directed by computer programs, or they may be

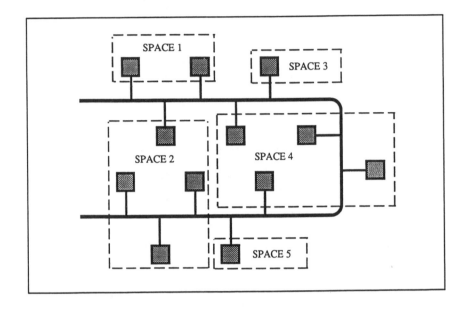

Figure 4. A network of 12 cyberspace decks participating simultaneously in five cyberspaces. Each deck maintains a complete copy of the space in which it participates. To minimize network traffic, only state changes are communicated among decks (except at times, during construction tasks, when whole models are transmitted from one deck to another).

utterly undirected (inanimate). Sometimes you will know what is inhabited by whom (or what), but sometimes be surprised to find that objects, like trees or refrigerators previously assumed to be unintelligent, are, in fact, full of sophisticated abilities. This will bring cyberspace alive, giving it a magical and delightful (if spooky) quality.

The Virtual World of HDTV

Bret C. McKinney

High-Definition Television, or HDTV, has been hailed as a revolutionary innovation in telecommunications technology. It is also regarded as a dead-end technology, a transitional technology at best. The High-Definition Television industry at one time held the attention of State Department officials, innovators of technology, futurists, and even Wall Street speculators.

Over the last three to five years, an insurmountable amount of information has confounded both the public and industry's ideas and perceptions about the nature of HDTV. This information has been riddled with technological inaccuracy as well as uncertainty and bias. It is vital for the multimedia industry to dispel any preconceived notions about HDTV in order to gain an objective knowledge of what it is and is not. Placing HDTV in a contextual framework may help illustrate the nature of High-Definition Television technology.

By promoting HDTV as a retail consumer electronic device, manufacturers created an adverse image to HDTV's potential industrial markets. It is not just an improved television set for consumers, nor is it simply an enhanced image display technology. Unfortunately, these limited definitions of HDTV are what permeate the public, business, and industry perceptions. The reason is twofold: One, the nomenclature (the term *High-Definition Television*) identifies the technology as a new development for popular television, not an innovation in telecommunication systems or component technologies. Two, from the beginning, HDTV manufacturers targeted the broadcasting and entertainment industries. Manufacturers believed high-definition products would meet consumer and producer demands for higher-quality images and production. Recognizing that HDTV is not limited to the given terminology brings us closer to defining this nebulous technological innovation.

The computer industry has made enormous advances in image quality through both hardware and software. Identifying HDTV technology as a system of components incorporating both hardware and software draws us even closer to the perimeters that outline the nature of HDTV. Both computer and television technologies manage tremendous volumes of information and utilize both hardware and software to communicate the information in a *visual* environment. HDTV can facilitate the software and hardware capacities of computer technology; NTSC television technology cannot. HDTV systems can produce programs in real time for both broadcast and cable transmissions; computer systems cannot. Although there are elements in HDTV systems that can mediate between computer technology and television systems, HDTV still falls somewhere between and beyond the realms of these two powerful communication mediums. HDTV meets the criteria for programming, storing, retrieving and displaying information in a computer environment. By design, such systems produce, record, broadcast and display information all within an analog or digital domain.

Because HDTV encompasses innovations in both hardware and software, the broadest, yet most accurate and honest definition is: HDTV a quantitative innovation in *visual information technology.* Any technology, whether software or hardware, inherently capable of producing, recording, programming, storing, retrieving and transmitting images and visual information at 1000 line resolution or 1920 pixels per scan line, or above, qualifies as an innovative component technology within a *high-definition system* (HDS).

Resolving to address HDTV as an HDS (high-definition system) technology (or HDT, high-definition technology) allows brilliant multimedia innovations to participate in and contribute to advanced information and display technologies. This revised definition is long overdue and may, as a result, lead the HDTV, computer, and multimedia industries into isolation and protectionism. These measures have thwarted most efforts to establish a compatible U.S. standard in the industrial marketplace. Rapid realignment of economic players in the global arena are taking place while the United States gropes for an industrial policy. American-owned HDTV manufacturing may be out of reach, but taking a "leapfrog" approach with evolving and revolving technology will eventually bury American industry beneath foreign competition. If we are going to stay involved and competitive in the global arena, I believe it is of grave importance that the proponents and players in the visual information industries (e.g., MCC, M.I.T. Media Lab, Sarnoff et al) begin recognizing that as Wall Street entrepreneurs continue selling American-owned technology firms to Europe and Japan, their leading innovations in technology will become directed by the economic agendas of their foreign sponsors.

What Role Does an HDS Play in Virtual Reality Environments (VRE)?

Providing a breakdown of the primary technologies comprising a high-definition system will prove helpful in acquainting multimedia users with available HD technology. First, the hardware:

- *Display Technology* includes CRTs, TV monitors, liquid crystal displays (LCD), flat panel displays (FPD), and any other display mechanisms capable of 1000-line horizontal resolution or 1920 pixels per line.
- *Image Information Recording/Playback Technology* includes HD video tape recorder (VTR), HD videodisc/cassette recorder (VD/CR) and Integrated compact disc (CD-I, CD-ROM, DVI).
- *Information Delivery Technology* includes satellite distribution (DBS, KU-Band), microwave broadcast, cable transmissions, and fiber optic networks (ISDN). Conversion technologies are those tertiary innovations that provide interim or transfer services between various information mediums.
- *Image Information Conversion and/or Compression Technology* includes these hardware components: standards converters, telecines, electronic beam recorders (EBR), frame stores, and multiple sub-Nyquist sampling encoding (MUSE Systems). This hardware category is not intended to include all hardware technologies relevant to HD systems.

The software category primarily involves recording and programming mediums. They can be characterized as 1) storage and recording technology, including 35mm film, HD videotape (1″ and ½″), and digital disc storage technology; and 2) programming and image source technologies, which include real-time productions, computer-generated graphics and image/text information programs. Obviously, there are overlapping relationships between the various information mediums. The most important criteria for measuring the value of HD technology manifests in the display mechanisms.

The High-Definition Display Technology contains the following attributes under the SMPTE 240M standard:

1. Two times (2×) the vertical and horizontal resolution
2. Five times (5×) the visual detail
3. Ten times (10×) the color information
4. Additional picture brightness

5. Wide screen format 1:1.77 or 16:9 (aspect ratio)
6. Sound quality equivalent to compact disc (CD).

Under the 240M standard, the real-time image is displayed by an 1125 scanning line system on a 60Hz. cycle (30 fps) with a 2:1 interlace in a 16:9 screen format. The transmitted signal bandwidth is 30MHz of component RGB. These attributes reflect a comparison to the current NTSC standard 6MHz color signal which operates on a 525 scan line 2:1 interlace process on a 59.94Hz cycle. Often, when the 240M standard is discussed, potential user markets either do not relate to the standard's significance or they perceive the standard as a staid or compromised measure, and it is therefore a moot issue. Other standards and system configurations have been proposed, but the 1125/60 standard is the most progressive and comprehensive to date.

Although there are computer images being displayed on 2000-line resolution screens, and even up to 4000 lines, that not necessarily provides the research and development team with enough real-time response, a crucial element in virtual environments. The 240M standard equals a computer image displaying approximately 1.2 million pixels per screen. (1920 pixels per scan line) thus meeting the high-definition imaging criteria.

A high-definition system provides a number of significant technical advantages for VREs. Artificial environments require extensive amounts of memory to store the environment or setting. HDS can provide an alternative environment within its own digital storage medium. The natural relationship between fiber optics and HDS images allows for a higher resolution display environment, which promotes a greater transparency of the source technology. The advent of fiber optics makes it possible to project the full 30MHz signal into an HD receiver and display the visual information in a high-definition wide screen format. Fiber optics not only allows HD images to be output, they also work extremely well with HDS cameras for recording source material. The high volume of information being recorded and stored with fiber for high-definition VREs in no way compromises the integrity of the real-time video or the computer graphic images during playback. Having HD images promotes more accurate research in the areas of virtual and artificial reality, particularly in the area of object recognition.

By maintaining digital compatibility, manufacturers will be able to integrate and facilitate the needs of user markets. Digital components will also allow the users and researchers to access greater amounts of information without being overloaded with irrelevant information. This creates a conducive environment for hypertext and hypermedia.

Without high-definition digital imaging, virtual reality environments risk arriving at a stalemate waiting for the "leapfrog" proponents to comply with their demands for greater temporal and spatial resolution displays. To fully realize the technical significance of HDS within VREs, the multimedia industry must be willing to approach HDS manufacturers and be willing to understand the language, technology and agenda.

Implications for Virtual Reality

By beginning to look at the high-definition industry, pragmatists and leading researchers in virtual reality labs will find HD imaging is already in place at several multimedia sites. The prospective joining of these two information technologies could impel HD manufacturers and user markets to establish a competitive impetus capable of instituting a framework for United States industrial policy. Fortunately, the prime industrial markets are also the largest users of innovative visual information technology. The most aggressive users of some form of HD technology and multimedia systems are the Department of Defense, the medical industry, telecommunication markets, manufacturing plants (e.g., the auto industry), and swiftly moving up, the education and training facilities (e.g., classrooms and simulators).

Integrating HDS into virtual reality environments affords these potential markets applications never before available, much less thought of. Providing user markets with unprecedented application and utility of virtual reality enhanced by high-definition imaging in real time will undoubtedly create some diversion in the user's sense of realism. By examining the nature of the virtual reality application, we can determine the extent to which the technology can be productive. The factors surrounding the users' sense of realism include: 1) *Psychophysical* attributes that comprise the high-definition image, as well as the configuration of the VRE. 2) The *transparency* level of the technology regarding the application measures how aware the user is of the technologies creating the VRE. The users' potential application range from fiber optic hand gloves for video games to total body immersion in a simulated reality as in a flight simulator or the Lucas/Disneyland Star Wars amusement ride. Today, the psychophysical influences relegated to visual communication technology are determined primarily on our sense of sight and balance. The *transparency* level of virtual reality environments is still very low. Currently, this facet of virtual reality contends with two types of sensory perception. One involves bodily accessories, a hand glove and helmet with goggles and the other requires nothing more than a decision to be a passenger on a spaceship simulator and travel to the "Moon of Endor" at Disneyland. Both levels of simulation require conscious decisions to participate.

The current pursuits of institutions researching artificial reality focus primarily on VRE as entertainment vehicles or developing applications to "advance" the human condition. In the last three decades, our society was offered a cornucopia of remedies to enhance, advance, and romance the human soul. A number of years ago, the altruistic author of the human condition, Ray Bradbury, wrote a short story entitled "The Veldt." It was a story of two ambitious young children who entered a virtual reality environment within their own home only to have it end awry in a setting of their own creation. A fictional anecdote almost appears trite when addressing academe and industry.

As the innovations of visual information technologies surface for society's patronage, guidelines, checks and balances instituted for yesterday's innovations must be maintained. Any new technology that is developed and used without industry guidelines to govern its application and integration into targeted user markets must be given new guidelines and specifications. The temptation and dangers are far too great to allow widespread use of new developments to go unchecked. If there is any validity to questions concerning the opportunity for abuse and deception of popular visual media, let us be mindful of the *ABC Nightly News* program that staged a "virtual" stakeout to create "reality" while covering the Felix Bloch espionage story with a black-and-white video camera. Also, bear in mind the Middle East "combat" coverage staged by Dan Rather, *CBS Evening News* anchor in Afghanistan. Abuses by the national news networks, the most influential disseminators of "objective" free information and news, reveal that nothing is sacred and anyone is capable of violating the American public's trust. Regardless of the rudimentary technology abuses by the media and aside from their rationales, it is crucial that our society keep a system of checks and balances on the application and utility of emerging technologies. There has never been technology so capable of deceit and abuse than what is being developed in the visual information technology industries today, albeit in the name of peace. Ethics must be established and reinforced for these emerging technologies. The old regulations cannot prevent abuse, as shown previously. The U.S. Federal Government is not necessarily privy to these developments. This means that industry must and should be its own regulator.

In this decade, it is paramount that the lines of communication between information proponents and players remain open. The development of both virtual reality environments and high-definition systems

HDTV	High-Definition Television. Any production or delivery mechanism designed to display images in real time with 1000 lines of resolution or more.
HORIZONTAL RESOLUTION	The number of alternating b/w vertical lines that determine perceived detail across the width of the picture.
INTERLACE SCANNING	Vertically scanning images by alternating between the even and odd scan lines to create one frame. Expressed as a 2:1 ratio.
SDN	Integrated Services Digital Network. A universal telecommunications network consisting of optical fiber for the purposes of delivering digitized audio, real-time or still video, computer image and text data without regard to the information's quality, bandwidth or standard. The network is a service of the phone companies.
LUMINENCE	The brightness detail in the video signal.
MUSE	Multiple sub-Nyquist sampling encoding. A transmission scheme developed to sub-sample signals, thus requiring less bandwidth to transmit an HD image.
NTSC	National Television System Committee. The organization that established the standard for television production and broadcast. They set the current 525 scanning line per frame/frame per second standard.
PRODUCTION STANDARD	A set of guidelines set to insure production and broadcast equipment would be compatible for programming and delivery.

PROGRESSIVE SCANNING	A television scanning technique that scans images in a sequential order, thus creating a single frame with each complete vertical scan. Expressed as a 1:1 ratio.
RESOLUTION	The perceived image detail based on chroma, horizontal, diagonal, dynamic, temporal, spatial, and static resolution or qualities.
RF	Radio frequency. Identifies signals that are modulated on a carrier wave.
SPATIAL RESOLUTION	Image detail measured in the X, Y, Z axes. Also considered dynamic resolution.
TEMPORAL RESOLUTION	Measures image movements in time, not space. For example, if a ceiling fan is turning and you can see each blade as it turns and in which direction they are moving, then you have good temporal resolution. If the blades spin so quickly they appear to be going backward or stationary, then you have poor temporal resolution.
TRANSMISSION STANDARD	A set standard for transmitting and delivering signals to the home receiver. Not to be confused with Production Standards.
VERTICAL RESOLUTION	The number of alternating black-and-white lines that make up the perceived image detail from the top of the the screen to the bottom. Not to be confused with horizontal scanning lines.

may find a veritable link as the twentieth century comes to a close. Both technologies attempt to satisfy the users' sense of vision and thirst for information. As such developments take place, the maturity of each technology will be measured by its perceived degree of transparency to the user. Once the proper contextual framework is established between the multimedia industry and the high-definition technology industry, we can then begin to realize the true meaning of virtual reality.

Elements of a Cyberspace Playhouse

Randal Walser

Until recently, computer interface designers have regarded human beings as "users" of computers, and computers have been regarded as tools for the human mind. That view is now being challenged by an emerging paradigm that redefines the relationship between humans and computers. One manifestation of the new paradigm is an exciting new medium, cyberspace, that provides people with virtual bodies in virtual realities that emerge from simulations of three-dimensional (3-D) worlds. Building on a concept of cyberspace as a form of theater, this chapter describes the elements of a cyberspace playhouse for sports and fitness, a new kind of social gathering place where people go to participate in three-dimensional simulations.

Cyberspace is a medium that gives people the feeling they have been bodily transported from the ordinary physical world to worlds of pure imagination. Although artists can use any medium to evoke imaginary worlds, cyberspace carries the various worlds itself. It has a lot in common with film and stage, but is unique in the amount of power it yields to its audience. Film yields little power, as it provides no way for its audience to alter screen images. The stage grants more power than film does, as stage actors can "play off" audience reactions, but the course of the action is still basically determined by a script. Cyberspace grants seemingly ultimate power, as it not only enables its audience to observe a reality, but also to enter it and experience it as reality. No one can know what will happen from one moment to the next in a cyberspace, not even the spacemaker (designer). Every moment gives each participant an opportunity to create the next event. Whereas film depicts a reality to an audience, cyberspace grants a virtual body and a role, to everyone in the audience.

The premise of this chapter is that cyberspace is fundamentally a theatrical medium, in the broad sense that it, like traditional theater, enables people to invent, communicate, and comprehend realities by "acting them out."[8] Acting within this point of view is not just a form of expression, but a fundamental way of knowing. To act is to become someone else in another set of circumstances, thereby requiring a person to know and experience a different reality. By giving his body over to a character, an actor enters a character's reality, and he or she can be said to embody (that is, provide a body for) the character. The character lives through the actor but so, too, does the actor live through the character. An actor in cyberspace is no different, except that the body he or she gives to her character is not a physical body, but rather a virtual one. One embodies the character but is also embodied by cyberspace.

A group of people is the first ingredient of theater, so some way must be provided for cyberspace patrons to gather in one place. Of course, in principle there is no need for patrons to assemble in the same physical space, as high-speed data communication channels can be used to bring them together in imaginary places. The day may come when people can enter cyberspace from their own homes, or perhaps from any location (just as it is now possible to place a phone call from any vehicle within a cellular phone grid). Meanwhile, the infrastructure of cyberspace is bulky and expensive enough to warrant a physical gathering place. I sketch out some possible elements of such a place, a new kind of social center, called a cyberspace playhouse, where people go to play roles in simulations.

While playhouses will be used for many purposes, including drama, design, education, business, fitness, and fun, this chapter describes a playhouse which emphasizes sports and physical conditioning. Cyberspace will turn out to be best suited to social activities that engage not just the mind but the whole body and spirit.

Sport is related to theater in that both are refined forms of play. Whereas theater evolved out of the human impulse to pretend, and thus to plan, sport evolved from the human impulse to assert the self, thereby ensuring survival. Actors perform in order to be someone else. Athletes act in order to be fully themselves. Sport, in a sense, is a contrivance, a ritualized pretext for being and acting. It gives people a reason to experience their bodies, to become physically alive. In other application areas it may not be so easy to imagine what good can come from giving people virtual bodies. But the relevance of the whole human body to sport is obvious. In order for people to play sports in cyberspace we must squarely face and solve the central problem of cyberspace, the ways and means of embodiment.

New Paradigm

If one were to dissect the elements of cyberspace technology it might appear that cyberspace offers nothing really new. Indeed, many of the key elements, most notably computer graphics, have been around a long time. What is new about cyberspace is not so much the underlying technologies, but the way they are packaged and applied to human activities. Cyberspace is a medium that is emerging out of a new way of thinking about computers and their relationship to human experience. Under the old way of looking at things computers were regarded as tools for the mind, where the mind was regarded as a disembodied intellect. Under the new paradigm, computers are regarded as engines for new worlds of experience, and the body is regarded as inseparable from the mind.

The new perspective on human-computer interaction is due in part to recent advances in computer graphics and simulation, and in part to reductions in the cost of key user interface technologies. The new perspective was precipitated, though, by the growing realization in the scientific community that the basis of rationality is not in the world, as had been supposed, but in the human body. The essence of this new view is expressed eloquently in five words, in the title of Mark Johnson's book, *The Body in the Mind*. In the introduction, Johnson lays out the fundamental tenets of the emerging paradigm, as follows:

> *We human beings have bodies. We are 'rational animals,' but we are also 'rational animals,' which means that our rationality is embodied. The centrality of human embodiment directly influences what and how things can be meaningful for us, the ways in which these meanings can be developed and articulated, the ways we are able to comprehend and reason about our experience, and the actions we take. Our reality is shaped by the patterns of our bodily movement, the contours of our spatial and temporal orientation, and the forms of our interaction with objects. It is never merely a matter of abstract conceptualizations and propositional judgments.[5]*

In another time or in another society, Johnson's comments might seem obvious, even trivial. But in a society built on a philosophical and scientific tradition that elevates mind over body, his point of view is heresy of the highest order, for it challenges the presupposition that the world is inherently rational, the basis for the very notion of a mind apart from a body.

Under the classical scientific view there is no need to give a place to the human body in any account of human reason because the classical view presupposes the existence of an objective reality with a rational structure. Reason is treated as a purely abstract system for converging step by step on the one correct description of the world. Under the new view, however, the world is not assumed to have a rational structure, and there is no sense in trying to find one. Instead, there are many possible worlds, as many as sentient beings can invent and experience. Nothing, under the new view, is meaningful until it has been experienced, either by the body, or by the "body in the mind" (that is, the body-related "schema" in the mind, that organize and guide behavior).

Definition of Cyberspace

There is cyberspace the communications medium, and then there is cyberspace the phenomenon. Cyberspace as a phenomenon is analogous to physical space. Just as physical space is filled with real stuff (so we normally suppose), cyberspace is filled with virtual stuff. Cyberspace, the medium, enables humans to gather in virtual spaces. It is a type of interactive simulation, called a *cybernetic simulation*, which gives every user a sense that he or she, personally, has a body in a virtual space. Just as cybernetic simulation is a special kind of interactive simulation, a *cyberspace*, the phenomenon, is a special kind of virtual space, one that is populated by people with virtual bodies.

Roots

Visionaries have discussed and promoted the essential aspects of cyberspace, under various names, since the 1960s. The roots of the field are generally traced to Ivan Sutherland and his seminal work on "Sketchpad," the first widely known interactive computer graphics system.[15] Sutherland described a head-mounted three-dimensional display as early as 1968.[16] Another evolutionary line can be traced to the same period, to Douglas Engelbart and his efforts to augment human intellect.[2] Much later, Papert spoke of "microworlds," Krueger of "artificial reality," Brooks of "virtual worlds," Fisher and McGreevy of "virtual environments," Nelson of "virtuality," and Walker of "the world in a can."[12, 7, 1, 3, 11, 18] Indeed, the notion of projecting one's self into a virtual space is familiar to hackers throughout computerdom, from Unix masters who "move" deftly around the Unix file hierarchy, to adventure gamers who "fight" the forces of evil in imaginary worlds. The term "cyberspace" was first used by William Gibson in *Neuromancer*, to denote a global computer/communications network supporting "consensual hallucinations" involving billions of people on a daily basis.[4]

Today the emerging field is variously referred to as cyberspace, artificial reality, and "virtual reality," the term favored by Jaron Lanier, one of the most visible of the field's advocates.[6] Whereas Lanier would use "virtual reality" to refer both to a virtual space and experiences within the space, I distinguish a special kind of virtual space, a cyberspace, which promotes experiences involving the whole body. The distinction might seem obtuse, at first thought, but it is no different in principle from the distinction between film, for example, and the apparent realities expressed through film (i.e., between "filmic space," on the one hand, and "virtualities" communicated via film on the other).

Theatrical Conception

As a form of theater, *cyberspace* can be regarded as a computer-based medium that enables groups of people to play the roles of characters in cybernetic simulations of three-dimensional worlds: crucially, cyberspace gives the role players the ability to sense a virtual reality from the point of view of the characters they play.

The term *world* in the ordinary sense refers to a three-dimensional euclidean space in which objects obey certain fundamental and predictable laws of behavior and organization (similar to "laws of nature"). A *virtual reality* is a consensual reality that emerges from an interactive simulation such as SIMNET[17] or Maze Wars+[10] in contrast to a consensual reality that emerges from the ordinary physical world). By *consensual reality* I mean the world, or a simulation of a world, as viewed and comprehended by a society.

A *character* is a being with a virtual body in a virtual reality. The role of a character is played by an *intellect,* either a human (called a *patron* or sometimes just a *player*) or an artificial intelligence program (called an *AI*). A virtual object that embodies an intellect is referred to as a *puppet,* to emphasize that it is directed by a role player. Since an intellect plays the role of a character, a character can be said to be embodied by a puppet (which is to say, a puppet embodies both an intellect and a character). A puppet that embodies a human intellect is referred to as a *droid* (as in "android") and a puppet that embodies an AI is called a *bot* (as in "robot"). Sometimes the controlling intellects themselves are loosely referred to as droids or bots.

A virtual reality is "consensual" in that its players have agreed, explicitly or implicitly (by virtue of their participation), to relate to it in the same way, to "play fair." But the reality is constructed through an organic process of give and take among the players, whether through cooperation, conflict, negotiation, compromise, agreement, force, abstention, or whatever.

Were it not for the stipulation that cyberspace be computer-based, the definition would admit many common forms of theater, sports, and games. As it stands, the definition includes many computer-based simulation games and training devices. It does not, however, include most computer-aided design (CAD) systems for three-dimensional modelling. While three-dimensional computer graphics are fundamental to cyberspace technology, most 3-D CAD systems do not provide their users an embodiment in virtual space—nor even, in most cases, a first-person view of a space.

There are some who consider head-mounted visual displays to be requisite equipment for the true experience of cyberspace, but head-mounts are just one means to an end (though an especially effective means). What matters is the extent to which players are able to suspend their disbelief in the illusion that they inhabit bodies apart from their physical bodies. The sole purpose of cyberspace technology is to trick the human senses and sensibilities, to help people believe and sustain an illusion. Head-mounted visual displays are important because they flood the human sense of sight with illusory images, making it much easier for most people to suspend their disbelief. Nonetheless, head-mounted displays are merely one means among many, including out-the-window visual displays, three-dimensional audio displays, motion platforms, force-feedback devices, credible simulation worlds, dramatic tension, high stakes, engaging stories, and social reinforcement. The upshot is that there is no surefire way to put people into cyberspace; ultimately, the job is an artistic one.

Art of Spacemaking

The goal of a spacemaker is basically the same as the goal of a playwright, a filmmaker, or any other creative artist. In *The Seven Stages of Theatre*, Richard Southern describes art as ". . . an address (in some form) by an individual to a number of people."[14] He is careful to point out that the art is not in the address, but in the manner of address. As he says, art is the process of saying something and meaning something else.

What creative artists do depends critically on the relation of their medium to their audience. A playwright creates a set of instructions for enactment by skilled actors performing before an audience. A filmmaker does basically the same thing (often with the help of a screenwriter, a kind of playwright), except what is presented is not a performance, but rather a recording of one. In either case, the audience observes a reality but never participates directly in it.

Whereas the playwright and the filmmaker both try to communicate the idea of an experience, the spacemaker tries to communicate the experience itself. A spacemaker sets up a world for an audience to act directly within, and not just so the audience can imagine they are experiencing an interesting reality, but so they can experience it directly. The filmmaker addresses the mind. The spacemaker addresses the body, and thereby the mind as well.

It is vital for the spacemaker to remember that a virtual reality is not just a computer-based simulation: it is a computer-based simulation played out by a group of people on a particular occasion. As I defined it earlier, a virtual reality is a special kind of consensual reality, one that is constructed from moment to moment by the spontaneous actions, and interactions, of the role players in a simulation. A virtual reality comes into existence when a group of people experience a simulation as if it were real—and that occasion, that one set of experiences, can happen only once. Thus the spacemaker can never hope to communicate a particular reality, but only to set up opportunities for certain kinds of realities to emerge. The filmmaker says "Look, I'll show you." The spacemaker says "Here, I'll help you discover."

In part, the job of the spacemaker is to design and construct worlds for players to experience, but that is merely the technical side of it. The more important part lies, as Southern says, in saying something and meaning something else. The art, in other words, is not in what the spacemaker constructs, but in the communication of insight which the spacemaker cannot construct (that is, some aspect of a deeper truth or higher reality).

Cyberspace Deck

In William Gibson's stories, cyberspace "cowboys" enter cyberspace by "jacking in" to an instrument called a "deck." The exact nature of a deck is never discussed, though it is clearly some sort of gateway through which people are transported to cyberspace. I use the term *deck* in the same sense, to refer to a physical space containing an array of instruments which enable a player to act within, and feel a part of, a virtual space.

Specifically, a cyberspace deck has seven components:

1. a *cyberspace engine* to generate a simulated world and mediate the player's interaction with it,

2. a *control space* (a box of physical space) in which the player's movements are tracked,

3. *sensors* to monitor the player's actions and body functions,

4. *effectors* to produce certain physical effects and stimulate the player's senses,

5. *props* to give the player solid analogs of virtual objects and vehicles,

6. a *network interface* to admit other players to the simulated world, and

7. an *enclosure* (or some sort of physical framework) to hold all the components.

Many decks will have just one prop, like a stationary bicycle, a railing, or a chair, and some decks will have no props at all.

Cyberspace Playhouse

A *cyberspace playhouse* is a place where people go, for various reasons, to play roles in cybernetic simulations. Its basic elements are modular cyberspace decks that are organized, and easily reorganized, according to the requirements of particular cyberspaces. Each playhouse has at least one *stage*, which is simply a physical area that encloses one or more cyberspace decks. Some playhouses will have many stages, with each one containing decks that have a similar form or function. Each deck is linked into a local area computer network (which may, in turn, be linked into a more global network).

A cyberspace is said to be a *multiplayer space* when it emerges from a simulation that is generated simultaneously by two or more decks. By the definition given above, a cyberspace must have at least one human player (since a cyberspace emerges from a cybernetic simulation, which embodies a person), but the other players can be AI programs running on decks that are not being used by humans. If the multiplayer space involves two or more humans then the space is called a *multiperson space*.

If cyberspace decks can be made modular enough, and portable enough, it will be easy to equip a playhouse for practically any kind of cyberspace. In principle, a cyberspace playhouse could be used for everything from drama and sports to design, education, games, product promotion, planning, job training, and sensational parties. In practice, each playhouse will be limited by the types of decks it contains. If a cyberspace requires a certain type of deck, which a playhouse does not have, then the playhouse will not be able to "run" the cyberspace at that particular time. To put it the other way around, a playhouse can run a cyberspace if 1) the house has the cyberspace in its (software) library, 2) it has the types of decks the space requires, and 3) a deck is available for at least one participant. It is easy to imagine that some playhouses will specialize to the point that they rarely, if ever, run new spaces, and never replace their decks, while other playhouses will offer a steady stream of new spaces that run for periods of weeks or months, like movies or theater productions.

Since each deck is capable of running a complete cybernetic simulation, a playhouse with 20 decks can run 20 spaces simultaneously. Or, at the other extreme, if every player chooses to join the same space, the playhouse will run just that one space, and all 20 players will be inside.

Sports and Fitness Playhouse

The critical thing to realize about the design of cyberspaces, for sports, is that sporting decks will generally have sophisticated props, like recumbent bicycles and inclined treadmills, and that sporting houses will make money by renting time on those decks. The purpose of a cyberspace for sports is not just to help people have fun and stay fit. It is also to help keep sporting houses in business, by keeping their decks full of players. If sporting houses are to be economically viable, then the spaces they run must 1) give patrons good reasons to rent time on decks, and 2) be organized so as to keep every deck constantly in use, but without making patrons wait inordinately long for decks to become available.

A sporting house could be used for many purposes, including physical training, survival games (like capture-the-flag), races, tours, rallies, various forms of dance, tournaments, adventure games, orienteering, and variations on traditional sports like baseball and racquetball. It might be located in any number of places like a school or university, a training camp, a shopping mall, a corporate office building, a hotel, or an amusement park. The kind of sporting house I have in mind emphasizes fitness and is modelled on circuit training, a conditioning regimen consisting of an alternating sequence of aerobic (steady) and anaerobic (explosive) exercises. A typical sporting house of this kind might be located in a converted fitness center and have eleven stages: four for dancing, two for lifting, and one each for cycling, rowing, climbing, skiing, and running/walking. If each stage has four decks, the playhouse would hold 44 decks in all. That means it could accommodate a total of 44 (local) patrons at a time (though data links to other playhouses might allow much larger player pools).

In order to control traffic and guarantee the availability of decks, the visits of patrons must be carefully scheduled and planned. Since a circuit requires a number of fitness machines, generally one for each exercise, it is important that sporting houses be designed to periodically pull players along from one deck (exercise station) to another. Fortunately, since cyberspace playhouses will be extensively wired and computerized, patrons can be tracked and guided individually. This is useful not just for traffic control, but also as the basis for personalized games and workout programs. On the other hand, the goal of the spacemaker (under the theatrical approach) is not just to foster personalization, but also socialization. The goal is not to equip people to disappear into their own private realities (desirable as that may be, for some purposes), but to help individual patrons participate in public realities with other living beings.

A sporting house, then, is construed to be an enterprise that rents out time in *public* cyberspaces. These are living environments that patrons may visit just as if they were public parks or recreation centers. A cyberspace has a life of its own, in other words, independently of individual humans. This does not imply that a cyberspace can exist independently of humans. According to the definition above, a cybernetic simulation must involve at least one human. A space, in a sporting house, functions like a real place, and while it cannot exist independently of human participation, neither does it end when the last patron leaves; it simply pauses until another patron enters. Thus, while a cyberspace is an evolving environment, it changes only when there is at least one patron jacked into it. This might be an ontological hedge, but it is also a practical necessity: in order for a cyberspace to continue unfolding without a human to experience it the playhouse would have to continue running the underlying simulation S; and that, if all decks are running simulations other than S, would require more computing power than the playhouse could muster (assuming it has no computers other then those in its decks).

Since a training circuit is a sequence of activities at successive exercise stations, it seems natural to set up a correspondence between the activities and the segments of a path or course in a cyberspace. For example, a simple circuit that calls for running, rowing, and cycling might correspond to a course with three legs: a running trail, a lake, and a highway. The player would then use a treadmill to run along the trail, a rowing machine to cross the lake, and a stationary bicycle to pedal down the highway. In general, a workout in cyberspace could be regarded as similar, conceptually, to the traversal of an obstacle course in the physical world. This conception is appealing in its simplicity, but unfortunately it is too simple to be viable in an actual sporting house. The problem is that decks are shared resources, and if there is a high demand then a particular deck may not be available when a particular player needs it. It is not reasonable to expect a player to wait on a bicycle, for example, after running a trail and rowing across a lake. By the time a bicycle becomes available the player may have rested long enough to negate, or at least diminish, the benefits of the workout.

A commercial playhouse that is open to the public can no more guarantee the availability of a deck than a movie theater can guarantee a seat, at a particular time, to everyone who wants to see a popular movie. The best one can hope for is a strategy that minimizes inconvenience without unduly compromising the service the playhouse is designed to provide. One such strategy is to allow variability in the sequence of training activities. That is, a player would specify the activities she wishes to perform, but not necessarily in any order. Instead, she would rely on the playhouse to route her to available decks, whatever they may be, as long as they are members of the set of decks she has selected. In fact, varying the sequence of activities is considered good practice by trainers and coaches, because athletes are quite good (subconsciously) at learning the path of least resistance through a regular exercise program.[13] Thus, varying the sequence of activities not only increases the opportunity to resolve scheduling conflicts, but also precludes the opportunity to minimize effort (and benefit).

Unfortunately, if a player can move in any order from one deck to another, then it is no longer possible to maintain a neat correspondence between physical activities and features in a virtual terrain. If a spacemaker knows, for example, that running will always be followed by rowing, then he can arrange for a running trail to lead to a boat dock on a lake. But, what if no rowing machine is available to a player when she reaches the virtual dock? What if a bicycle is all that is available? Is she supposed to pedal the bike across the lake? Anything is possible in cyberspace, even bicycles that skim over water or fly through the air, but well-constructed cyberspaces, like well-crafted plays and movies, will not rely on magic to repair conceptual flaws. The flying bicycles in the movie *E.T.*, for example, are not merely contrivances that enable plot transitions, but an integral part of the story.

It might be better, in the circuit training example, to provide a virtual boat that is pedaled instead of rowed across the lake, especially if the available prop is a recumbent bicycle. In that case it should be as easy for the player to believe she is sitting in a boat as on a bicycle. On the other hand, if the prop is a standard racing bicycle, then there will probably be a mismatch between the way the player moves in physical space and the way her puppet moves in cyberspace (since, presumably, she is sitting in a basically upright position in physical space while her character is reclining in cyberspace). A mismatch of this sort might be described as *kinesthetic dissonance,* and should be avoided, in general, because it informs the body that something is "out of whack," and can break the illusion that the virtual world is real.

Another approach would be simply to provide an entirely different space for every activity (as opposed to a different space for every workout program). Thus, there would be a space for bicycles, a space for rowboats, a space for skis, and so on. There would not be as much variety in each space, but there would be no problem matching players' physical activities and props with virtual counterparts. The transition from one deck to another would correspond to a "hyperjump" from one space to another.

Still another approach would be to set up a correspondence between exercises in the physical world and sporting events, like races and lifting contests, in a single virtual space. Unlike activities on an obstacle course, there would be no need for any of the sporting events to take place in contiguous locations. When a player moves from one deck to another his character would make a hyperjump to the starting location of the next event. Although events would not need to occur contiguously, there is no reason why they should not, and in fact they might even overlap in virtual space; thus, a bicycle race might occur on the same road as a foot race, and avoiding collisions with other players (or intentionally causing collisions) might be part of the challenge. To insure the periodic rotation of players from deck to deck, a time limit might be imposed on each event. If each event lasted ten minutes, then a player could rotate through six different major activities in an hour. Even if the playhouse were at capacity, the first "wave" of queued players would have to wait no more than ten minutes to begin their circuits.

Conclusion

Over a quarter century ago, Marshall McLuhan said that electric technology is bringing us rapidly to ". . . the final phase of the extensions of man—[to] the technological simulation of consciousness, when the creative process of knowing will be collectively and corporately extended to the whole of human society. . . ."[9] It was difficult, then, to imagine quite what McLuhan was talking about, but today the "final phase" could well be at hand, in the form of an emerging medium called cyberspace. Does cyberspace represent the final extension McLuhan had in mind? It is still too early to tell, but the important question is not what cyberspace is, today, but rather what it can become.

McLuhan's great insight was that to understand a medium, one must understand its message (as opposed to its content), and the message of any medium is the "change of scale or pace or pattern that it introduces into human affairs." We have the opportunity today, to make whatever we want of cyberspace. To do so we must decide what message we want it to convey; which is to say, we must imagine how we want it to change human affairs. Today, a cyberspace playhouse is only a thought experiment, but it could soon be the infrastructure that makes us whole again, by bringing us back to our bodies. It is hard to imagine that any enterprise, or any medium, could have a more profound effect on human affairs.

Notes

This paper is based upon "Elements of a Cyberspace Playhouse," in *Proceedings of the National Computer Graphics Association 1990, Anaheim, California, March 19-22, 1990.* Published by NCGA.

1. Brooks, F.P. (1988) Grasping reality through illusion: interactive graphics serving science. ACM SIGCHI.

2. Engelbart, D.C., Watson, R.W., and Norton J.C. (1973) The augmented knowledge workshop. *Proc. National Computer Conference.*

3. Fisher, S.S., McGreevy, M., Humphries, J., and Robinett, W. (1986) Virtual environment display system. ACM 1986 Workshop on Interactive 3-D Graphics, University of North Carolina, Chapel Hill, North Carolina.

4. Gibson, W. (1984) *Neuromancer.* New York: Ace Books.

5. Johnson, M. (1987) *The Body in the Mind: The Bodily Basis of Meaning, Imagination, and Reason.* Chicago: The University of Chicago Press.

6. Kelly, K. (1989) "Virtual Reality: An Interview with Jaron Lanier." *Whole Earth Review.* No. 64. pp. 108-119.

7. Kreuger, M. (1982) *Artificial Reality.* Addison- Wesley.

8. Laurel, B. (1989) On dramatic interaction. *Verbum* 3.3. pp. 6-7.

9. McLuhan, M. (1964) *Understanding Media: The Extensions of Man.* New York: Signet Books.

10. McNeil, A., Sloane, B., Fenton, J., and Neumann, E. (1986) *Maze Wars+.* A simulation game from MacroMind, Inc.

11. Nelson, T. (1987) *Computer Lib.* 2d ed. Redmond, WA: Microsoft Press. (First ed. publ. in 1974).

12. Papert, S. (1980) *Mindstorms: Children, Computers, and Powerful Ideas.* New York: Basic Books, Inc.

13. Sobey, E. and Burns, G. (1982) *Aerobic Weight Training Book.* Runner's World Books.

14. Southern, R. (1961) *The Seven Ages of the Theatre.* New York: Hill and Wang.

15. Sutherland, I. (1963) Sketchpad, a man-machine graphical communication system. Ph.D. Thesis, Massachusetts Institute of Technology.

16. Sutherland, I. (1968) A head-mounted three-dimensional display. FJCC. Vol. 33, pp. 757-764.

17. Thorpe, J.A. (1987) The new technology of large scale simulator networking: implications for mastering the art of warfighting. Ninth Interservice Industry Training Systems Conference.

18. Walker, J. (1988) Through the looking glass. Internal paper. Autodesk, Inc., Sausalito, California.

Designing Realities: Interactive Media, Virtual Realities, and Cyberspace

Joseph Henderson

Well-executed simulations should provide a sense of having had a life experience: learning occurs at an essential level where a fundamental change in attitudes and behavior occurs. To help accomplish this, we have worked very hard to create realities that are rich in concepts, that are realistic in content and in their portrayal of physical and social environments, that are interesting and entertaining to use[1,2,3]. Another specialty is providing physical and cognitive access to large, multimedia databases[4,5]. These two interests are related in that they are concerned with the presentation and representation of information to people who need to make decisions, either now (decision-assistance for patients, clinicians, researchers, administrators) or in the future (education and training).

Interactive media design is the marshalling of technological tools to organize the presentation of visual, auditory and textual information, creating a conceptual environment in which people can learn. Design is the single distinguishing feature of interactive media, setting it apart from standard audio-visual, or even "straight computer-assisted learning," programs; design defines interactive media. Assuming all other elements meet conventional "production value" standards, design is *the* critical determinant of success or failure of an interactive media program. This important issue is often neglected as we rush to develop new concepts and technologies for communicating information.

The terms *virtual reality,* and *cyberspace* describe new developments that extend our concept of interactive media. Much of our experience in designing interactive media simulations is applicable to designing virtual realities; similarly, work with multimedia databases is applicable to designing cyberspace environments. This chapter will illustrate these concepts by discussing two projects: Regimental Surgeon and Traumabase. However, before this discussion, it is essential to define our terms.

Interactive multimedia places the retrieval and display of information under the control of a computer program and the user. It allows the simultaneous and integrated display of information in four forms (listed with some examples from medicine):

- *Text and numbers:* data that are raw (medical histories, monitor readouts, vital signs) and reduced (case summaries, tables, statistics).
- *Images:* computer-generated or video, still or moving, superimposable on a single monitor (monitor readouts, graphic or video representation of patient signs and symptoms, X-rays, cardiograms, videotapes of patients and other care providers).
- *Sounds:* foreground sounds (histories, physiological sounds, conversation or verbal requests from other care providers) and background sounds (devices such as respirators and monitors, other environmental sounds).
- *Models:* of processes pertinent to the subject being taught; ultimately, these are conceptual models of the way things are or should be. They can be expressed as algorithms or procedural specifications, or as mathematical or spreadsheet models (body compartments and drug uptake/release, physiological response to hemorrhage, wound ballistics, probability models of clinical complications, economic models of care systems).

Virtual realities are a multimedia environment that provides users a sense of participating in realities different from their own. The main purpose of virtual realities is to provide experiences that are transferable to, and enrich our everyday, non-virtual reality. As such, they are equivalent to high-fidelity simulations produced using interactive media or with specialized systems such as aircraft simulators. According to some designers, virtual realities and cyberspace are interchangeable terms which require a "bodily" participation using specialized hardware such as head-mounted displays, hand or body position sensors, and kinesthetic feedback units. This chapter contends that realities and cyberspace are different (though closely related) and do not require participation of the physical body. The interactive media program Regimental Surgeon is an example of a virtual reality.

Cyberspace originated in the fiction of William Gibson. Gibsonian cyberspace is a decidedly non-physical "matrix," with abstract geometries representing the relationships between data systems. Its main purpose is to provide access to information. Gibson describes cyberspace as

A consensual hallucination experienced daily by billions of legitimate operators, in every nation, by children being taught mathematical concepts . . . A graphic representation of data abstracted from the banks of every computer in the human system. Unthinkable complexity. Lines of light ranged in the nonspace of the mind, clusters and constellations of data. Like city lights, receding, . . .[6]

As defined above, cyberspace addresses an extremely knotty problem in interactive media design: how to represent vast quantities of information existing in a variety of forms, and allow exploration and navigation of contained information. A recent announcement of the First Cyberspace Conference stated that:

. . . the nature of cyberspace conceived of as an independent realm, a shared virtual environment whose objects and spaces are data, visualized (and heard) . . . It also seeks to reach an understanding of how the components of cyberspace already ''under construction'' . . . might someday function together to create a true, public cyberspace, as well as private, special-purpose cyberspaces: viable, 3-dimensional, alternate realities providing the maximum number of individuals with the means of communication, creativity, productivity, mobility, and control over the shapes of their lives within the new information and media environment.[7]

The Traumabase project is an early example of a cyberspace environment.

Virtual Reality: "Regimental Surgeon"

Description of the Program

Regimental Surgeon is a Level III interactive media program (using an attached microcomputer) intended for U.S. Navy physicians. This program was developed for the Naval Health Sciences Education and Training Command as part of the Navy's Computer-Assisted Medical Interactive Video System. "Regimental Surgeon" is a 'microworld' simulation which the user can enter, explore, discover facts, and formulate rules and principles much as an individual would in real life. The program is intentionally entertaining as well, placing the learner within the context of a story whose evolution and outcome depend on the decisions made by the learner. Numerous themes are developed simultaneously, any of which can be developed and emphasized in discussions outside the context of the program itself.

The program has the following objective: To provide, through simulation, experiences which will allow the learner to develop knowledge and skills needed to function as a staff medical officer in a hypothetical combat scenario involving the U.S. Marine Forces. In the process, the learner is challenged to:

1. Evaluate and define the medical threat (malaria) confronting Marine Forces in his unit.
2. Identify, plan, and implement the preventive medicine countermeasures which can reduce risk.
3. Communicate the urgency of those countermeasures to key commanders.

There are ten other facilitating objectives dealing with basic organizational, interpersonal, and medical aspects of functioning as a staff medical officer.

Design Issues

The program is organized loosely as an 'adventure' computer game in which various locations can be visited. In such a game, the locations can contain treasures and/or characters with which limited interactions can occur. In Regimental Surgeon the locations are various elements and units of the Regiment (Headquarters and the three Battalions), Division Headquarters, and medical support units (hospitals); the "treasures" are facts which can be obtained from a variety of sources in a variety of ways: epidemiologic surveys, reading documents, questioning individuals, and looking at blood smears. The learner is required to assemble the facts acquired, draw conclusions, and subsequently inform and make recommendations. Characters can facilitate or obstruct this process or act as mentors, depending on the learner's actions.

The program begins with an *Opening Sequence* that sets the scenario, introduces most of the main characters, and establishes principal rules of the game. It is also intended to engage the learner and serve as a motivating influence to continue and complete the simulation.

Midgame contains the core of the program. There are 40 scenes of two types: initial and developmental. Initial scenes are those seen by the learner on the first visit while developmental scenes further plot development and reflect learner's progress to that point. During development there are up to three encounters with each of eight main characters (of a total of 32 speaking parts). There are different versions of the encounters for seven of the characters, encouraging/friendly or distracted/distant or unfriendly, depending on how the learner has handled the job so far. Each character, representing main teaching points, has a different view on the learner's job and how it should be performed. Response from the other principal character (the chaplain) is constant for each of the encounters although the dialogue depends on the learner's previous choices.

Epilogue is a coda to wrap things up. If the learner has managed to keep Division out of problems and has delivered the briefing, an opportunity is provided to back up assertions with evidence; feedback depends on completeness of investigation and plan. If Division did get involved, then a different ending is seen.

In general, this program is designed to train rather than educate. To an extent this training teaches domain-dependent facts (rather than domain-independent definitions and general theorems), and usually involves learning from mentors and experience (heuristically, rather than from formal lectures and textbooks). This program teaches through experience by putting the learner "on-the-job," in this case, as a Regimental Surgeon in a combat zone. Instead of a didactic approach, the learner acquires knowledge through a series of interactions with mentors and situations that depend on the choices he or she makes traversing the program. This experiential learning approach is similar to role-playing games and exercises used in military and business schools.

Since there are many ways to traverse the program, the learner can gather information in ways and to an extent that is variable (the role of chance is minimized by placing critical information redundantly). For example, the learner may choose to play a very active role, traveling personally throughout the command, gathering needed information and completing the program in a very comprehensive (perhaps too comprehensive) and successful way; or the participant may delegate some of the work and play a less active role, and still be successful; he or she could even choose to stay in a tent or sleep to produce unsuccessful outcome. In each case the learner experiences the consequences of personal actions, and learns whatever is decided is the knowledge contained therein. Thus, instructional content is variable in two ways: it depends on the path chosen by the student and it depends on the student's interpretation of the events encountered on the path.

Finally, representing contained information is an interface design issue addressed by what some call a "concept map." Concept maps in Regimental Surgeon are literally a series of nine animated maps to provide a means of navigating through the physical, temporal, and conceptual elements of this reality. Upon reaching a location, the user is presented a "talk" menu to allow questions or read documents, blood smears, or tactical maps. A design goal that the interface be intuitive, i.e., a user would not require additional instruction, was met in two ways:

- By using logical design, in the sense that graphics and content are consistent and integrated with the reality portrayed;
- By incrementally increasing the complexity of the interface, starting with simple menus and adding features.

A Cyberspace Environment: Traumabase

Description of Traumabase

Gibson's ideas about cyberspace complement concepts of the emerging field of "scientific visualization," in which data and information are represented geometrically[8]. Traumabase applies these ideas to the study of war and war injury, using three-dimensional computer graphics to represent and access a vast public record, showing the realities of war in text, pictures, films, and sounds. The project is supported by the U.S. Army Medical Research and Development Command, and is being developed at the Casualty Care Research Center, Uniformed Services University of the Health Sciences.

A very large collection of data and information emerged from the Vietnam War. Some of that information has been compiled to help plan and teach about the medical care of casualties of war and similar disasters. The collection consists of some 200,000 sheets of paper (text descriptions, handdrawn diagrams and maps), over 50,000 35mm slides (casualties and their wounds, weapons and missiles, buildings, vehicles), hours of audio recordings (oral histories of casualties, care providers, planners), hours of film (documentary and training, showing evacuation, field care, surgical management), and a commercially-available videodisc history of the Vietnam War (*Vietnam: the 10,000 Day War*). All of this information is in the process of being stored and catalogued electronically for access, retrieval, and manipulation via a Macintosh II computer, magnetic disk and optical disc (CD-ROM and videodisc) storage.

Design Issues

Because this multimedia database is large and complex, cognitive access is limited by our ability to adequately represent the information it contains. This is a general problem: with conventional approaches, using lists and indices, information elements become structured in ways that impose cognitive barriers. The usual, hierarchical structure conflicts with the associative thinking required as we struggle to achieve insight, understanding, and knowledge about the subject at hand. We cannot readily interact with data and information in the same way we think, moving rapidly and linking item to item, idea to idea, analysis to analysis. Traditional approaches lock analyses and minds to structures imposed by the system and the preconceptions of its creators.

The application of cyberspace and visualization concepts can allow us to view data as a whole or in detail, to see elements in association with each other or individually, and to link those elements in association with each other or individually, and to link those elements to other information stored in a variety of media. New interfaces can be formed that depend on the current analysis, and not on the analyses and structures imposed by the creators of a data system.

To access and manipulate the Vietnam War database a computer graphic construct was created, representing contained information along important dimensions: location and severity of wounds, wound pattern clustering, wound pattern frequencies, survival patterns. This construct consists of a three-dimensional graphic matrix of integer values, an optimized projection of a six-space matrix; position and color of points and point complexes denote location and severity of wounds. This construct can be manipulated in several ways: rotation on three axes, zooming, highlighting, masking or slicing on other variables. An effect is being able to travel through the matrix under mouse control, to different coordinates, regions and subregions[4].

Thus, the matrix can be explored and navigated: exploration to reveal expected and unexpected patterns and to identify interesting cases and case-complexes, navigation to return or direct others to known regions of interest in the matrix. Having explored or navigated the matrix, each region, subregion, or point can then be linked (via Hyper-Card or Acius 4th Dimension) to source data, allowing rapid retrieval, manipulation, and display of data, photographs, films, oral histories. An iterative and interactive process of discovery can result, in which the user interacts with the matrix and source data using the very powerful combination of eye, brain, and hand. This can provide a "visceral" sense or analysis of what the data have to tell us.

However, something more is going on here. Traditionally, dealing with databases has an intrinsically abstract nature. In the interest of "rational" or "scientific" decision-making we isolate the quantifiable and formulate models. A danger is that the abstraction can become the reality, and real world decisions can be made without due regard to the real world. However, in this system abstractions (the matrix) can be linked to increasingly concrete and emotionally powerful forms of information, to the realities of seeing people and hearing their stories. With this kind of approach we can involve the heart as well as the mind.

Designing Realities

We work in a complex and demanding media environment, and what we have learned that is good and useful has been hard-won. We are just discovering how to use the tools already available to us, much less emerging ones. Conceptual, software, and hardware tools—interactive multimedia, virtual realities, cyberspace, authoring environments, DVI, CDI, HMDs, DataGloves, and others we may not imagine—will just keep coming.

Ultimately, design is all about using the tools, irrespective of the tools themselves. A carpenter may know how to use a hammer, saw, chisel, and perhaps much more sophisticated tools, but ultimately it is what one does with the tools that counts. It is the same for designing realities: a worthy concept, attention to form and function, intelligent and esthetic employment of the talent and materials at hand, and commitment to quality in all aspects from the grand design to the smallest detail; those aspects mark the creations of great artists and artisans. We need more of these in our business.

Notes

1. Henderson, J., A. Galper, and W. Copes. "Interactive Videodisc to Teach Combat Trauma Care," *J. Med. Systems,* Vol. 10 (1986): 271–276.

2. Henderson, J. and A. Galper. "Interactive Video for Combat Trauma Care Training," in *MEDINFO 86, Proc. 5th World Congress on Med. Informatics,* Washington, DC, North-Holland, Amsterdam (Salmon and Blum, Eds.) (1986): 1115.

3. Henderson, J. "Regimental Surgeon: Interactive Media for Surrogate On-the-Job Training," *Proceedings of the Society for Applied Learning Technology,* Washington, DC, August 1989.

4. Henderson, J. "Cluster Analysis and Rotating 3-D Scatter Plots to Explore and Link a Multimedia Database," *Proc. 13th Symposium on Computer Applications in Medical Care, IEEE,* Washington, DC, (1989): 392–398.

5. Henderson, J. and J. Vayer. "Traumabase: A Multimedia/ Hypermedia System for Planning, Teaching, and Research in Combat

Casualty Care," *Proc. 13th Symposium on Computer Applications in Medical Care, IEEE,* Washington, DC, (1989): 1001–1004.

6. Gibson, W. *Neuromancer.* (New York: Ace Books, 1984), 51.

7. University of Texas at Austin School of Architecture. Call for abstracts: First Conference on Cyberspace. USENET Message-ID: 20731@utemx.UUCP , dated Nov 11, 1989.

8. McCormick, B., T. DeFanti, and M. Brown. "Visualization in Scientific Computing," *Computer Graphics* Vol. 21, no. 6. (November 1987) New York: ACM SIGGRAPH.

Fluxbase: A Virtual Exhibit

Joan S. Huntley
and Michael Partridge

Once totally disparate commodities, the distinctions between computers and art blur as they fuse together. Free associations with the word "computers" twenty years ago were "huge," "heavy," "exorbitant" and "number crunching"—at best, the subject of artistic derision. A decade later, perceptions changed to "big," "bulky," "expensive," "word processing" and "databases" and described as useful to museum staffs. Today, the computer is recognized as "lightweight," "portable," "affordable," a "multimedia development" platform and perceived as an increasingly indispensable tool for the artist. Currently, computer software for art is designed for those who need information about art, such as librarians and museum curators or those who create art, such as the artists themselves. Typically, a given software program benefits only one population.

This need not be the case. In a project underway at the Computer Assisted Instruction (CAI) Lab at the University of Iowa, we believe that it is not only possible, but indeed desirable, to create computer software useful to several populations working with art. Using a NeXT computer, we are developing Fluxbase, an application that blends traditional capabilities with new functions, defies categorization as a "database," "word processor," or "drawing tool," and meets the needs of many groups interested in contemporary art.

From Where Do We Speak?

Multiple, non-standard cataloging systems are used in museums and libraries to control information about alternative contemporary art. While accommodating the needs of curators and librarians, these systems fail to adequately represent the artists' intentions. In April 1989, Estera Milman, Curator of the Alternative Traditions in Contemporary Arts Archive at the University of Iowa, organized a planning conference, sponsored by the National Endowment for the Arts (NEA) to address problems with existing art networks and information systems. Based on our earlier work with videodisc-based computer systems for traditional Western art, we were invited to design a prototype to suggest how technology can help solve this problem.

Questions Guiding Our Design

Traditional architecture was used as a metaphor. A "contractor's special" is a common, no-frills, generalized blueprint. Yielding look-alike houses in many suburban subdivisions, this approach is easy and inexpensive, but fails to produce the best design for either the physical location or the buildings' inhabitants. By contrast, architecture "built-to-specification" is created with both the environment and inhabitants in mind. The same is true in designing computer-based programs; we aspired to design a program with the best fit for both the environment and consumers, as well as the various uses to be made of the program. In doing so, four questions guided the system design.

How Do Needs of Contemporary
(e.g., Fluxus) Art Collections Differ?

Indexing methods and retrieval designs should reflect the structure of the collection. The specific subset of contemporary art used in this prototype is "Fluxus." What is "Fluxus?" Definition and Fluxus are contradictory terms. It is impossible to state precisely when it started, or who was in it, or even what genre of art it is. The Fall 1979 issue of *lightworks* introduces Fluxus as

> . . . *a sort of alchemy. A box of broken watches, a deck of cards (each a two of spades), a concert performance of French Horns filled with ping-pong balls. It is the act and transformation of life into art . . . Be it performance art, the construction of boxes, the publishing, the festivals, this is a thoughtful and life-giving art . . . Yet no one is quite sure how to reckon with Fluxus, and the critics and the scholars have, for the most part, avoided doing so. Possibly because it is simply not one thing. The contents and form and contributors are diverse and disunited as the paradoxes are plentiful. Fluxus has no manifesto. It was hardly even a movement and Peter Frank aptly labels it a tendency. To be sure, it coalesced artists, designers, chemists, engineers, writers and more from all parts of the world in the early 1960s . . . is seminal in the development of happenings and performance art, concept art, artists' publishing, correspondence art and*

more. Ultimately Fluxus is renegade art, always on the fringe and continually defying tradition.

What, then, are the distinguishing aspects of Fluxus that should be addressed in our technological response? Let us examine the work Projects Class by David Askevold (ed.) as an example (shown in Appendix A).

Collaboration Among Artists

Flux artists collaborated significantly more than traditional artists. The collaborative tendency called for the artists to work together on individual artworks. *Projects Class* was a creation by 12 artists, each contributing a different card to the set. "Flux Year Box 2," the focal piece of our project, has at least seventeen contributing artists. This NeXT-based program needs to provide easy access to information about the multiple artists associated with a given work.

Understanding the Context

Many works of art are best understood in the context of the environment in which it was created, e.g., politics, religion, or even the artist's personal history, such as their physical and emotional states. Because Fluxus was a tendency rather than a well-defined movement, it is especially important to understand the events and environments in which Flux pieces were created. For example, in his article "Fluxus in New York," Peter Frank relates:

> *Higgins remembers Canal Street in the late 1950s and early 60s as an exciting, dynamic environment. The surplus stationers that predominated on the stretch of Canal between Centre Street and West Broadway were going out of business, and plastic surplus merchants and job lot dealers were replacing them. The little machines and objects available in these junk stores fascinated the artists in the neighborhood, including Higgins, Knowles, Lette Eisenhauer, and several Japanese including Ay-O, Yoko Ono, and Chieko Shiomi. It can be demonstrated that the visual aesthetic informing Fluxus work depends heavily on the objet trouve sensibility nurtured by the Canal Street atmosphere.*

Experiential as Well as Observational

Some art is best appreciated when visually observed in two dimensions such as the *Mona Lisa*. Three-dimensional art is often best appreciated when touched, or when the viewer moves around it such as a Henry Moore sculpture or when the viewer moves within it, e.g., Chartres Cathedral. Still other forms of art are best appreciated when the viewer manipulates it and experiences its three-dimensional unfolding over time. In "Projects Class," it would be intriguing to see the results of the projects and the photographs and texts reordered as instructed, not just the instructions alone.

Figure 1. Flux Year Box 2, unopened.

Several notable computerized databases embody these requirements. The most famous example of fluid and graceful control of a three-dimensional object is the Greek Vases videodisc at the Getty Museum of Art. At the University of Iowa, a HyperCard stack controlling a videodisc with 35,000 art images has been designed and developed in which the user can zoom in progressively closer to a view of a painting, rotate a piece of sculpture, and move across an architectural site. Over a decade ago M.I.T.'s Machine Architecture Group demonstrated "surrogate travel" through Aspen, Colorado. However, none of these projects embodied the sense of vicarious manipulation, the "virtual reality" component, users ought to experience when they open up *Flux Year Box 2* and play with its contents.

Material Relevant to the Works

Many Flux pieces were described on paper and then later produced from the descriptions, often by someone other than the artist; Projects Class is an example. These were created with such frequency that they acquired a name of their own: "artist's descriptions." Furthermore, since Flux works are contemporary creations, more printed information about these works (written by someone other than the artist) than exists for example, a work by Michelangelo. The system must incorporate both types of information: graphic and encoded using a bitmapped file or an analogue video signal, and as ASCII text.

Characteristics such as greater artist collaboration, a need to know the context, the amount of graphic and textual material related to an artwork do occur in traditional art forms, but they are far more prominent in Fluxus. It is an issue of magnitude, of the degree to which these features occur, rather than whether they exist at all. If a characteristic of an object in a database occurs once in three thousand instances, the computer may not need to accommodate it. But if the feature occurs in 2500 out of 3000 objects, the system design should reflect it.

Why Automate an Information Base in the Contemporary Arts?

Our original task was to create a system that would rectify the discrepancies among the diverse indexing methods used by librarians, museum conservators, and archivists.

For these user groups, the primary reason to automate is to gain additional and better quality information about works of art as well as facilitated referencing. Types of questions that could be answered include:

- did George Macunias create artists' books?
- where and when has a given artwork been exhibited/performed?
- where are artworks located today?
- which works of art sold for more than $50,000?
- how has the average price of artists' books changed over the past five years?

Solving this problem requires that the various parties maintaining information bases conform to a common set of data fields, terminology definitions, and protocols by which to share this information among the diverse systems that exist or will be created in the future. These are not trivial problems. Modifying a system that already exists may require changes in software and publications, new staff training, and last, but far from least, compromising on the form and function of the various fields of the information database. Many of the indexing systems and guidelines already in place have been carefully conceived and well executed. Some examples are the *Processing Manual* for the Franklin Furnace, a notable archive in New York, and the fields and procedures established by the Library of Congress. Yet, despite the richness of these adopted methods, they are dissimilar and in certain ways fail to capture the uniqueness of the artworks themselves. As we became more familiar with contemporary art, especially Fluxus, it became clear that the discrepancy between the form in which information was stored or retrieved and the spirit of the artists caused a greater problem. Describing non-traditional artwork with traditional data structures obscured much of its identity. Expanding the database to include graphic and audio data, and making this data available in a participatory rather than in a read-only form, demanded that we create a program providing not only information about, but also an understanding of and an appreciation for, the art. Questions which could then be answered include:

- how did the artist's performance sound?
- what does a certain work of art located across the continent look like?
- how did the piece work?

In short, experimenting with multimedia representations could yield a greater understanding of the artworks than restricted, textual data fields; its need is fairly obvious in the title of a 1984 exhibit catalog from Toronto's Art Metropole: *Evidence of the avant garde since 1957: selected works from the collection of Art Metropole including audio tapes, records, videotapes, film, multiples, kitsch, manuscripts, stamps, buttons, flyers, posters, correspondence, catalogues, porn, T-shirts, postcards, drawings, poems, mailers, books, photographs and ephemera.*

Whose Needs Are We Serving?

Librarians, curators, and archivists were well served by the original indexing system. However, contemporary artists also attended the NEA planning session. We believed we also needed to consider the interests and needs of contemporary artists, professors, students, curators, and librarians. Thus, we identified the following populations that varied in quality and quantity of their background knowledge; whether or not they wanted to correct, confirm or amplify the information; and whether or not they desired to have a more direct, experiential involvement with the art:

- administrator of an archive or library
- scholar/professor
- student
- original artist
- the community of artists

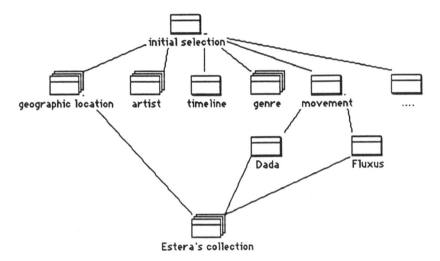

Which Universe Are We Modelling?

Having recognized potential users, the universe that was of greatest interest to each of these groups was identified as follows:

- administrator of an archive: the *local* collection
- scholar/professor: *worldwide* collection
- student: the *tendency* in general and the *artist* in particular
- original artist: their *own* works
- the community of artists: works in the same *genre*

Implementing the Design

Given that Fluxus was an international tendency, and that Flux art exists in collections all over the world, the system was designed to allow users to select artworks through several different conceptual entrances.

For example, using either traditional cartographic maps, or photographic clusters for the varying regions in the world, users will be able to select a geographic region. Because numerous networked computers were envisioned, users can narrow their visit to a single collection, e.g., one located in New York while they are in Los Angeles, creating a sort of virtual browsing. Alternatively, they may have a particular artist or genre already in mind.

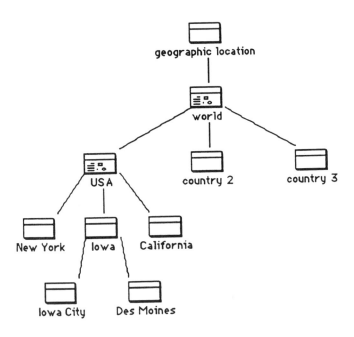

In short, a rich set of crosslinked information is created. This is not astoundingly new; it is mentioned to suggest richer sets of data as well as nontextual modes of inquiry.

Description of Prototype

Assuming the user has selected *Flux Year Box 2*, the closed box appears on the screen of the NeXT computer.

Clicking on the box, it opens to reveal its diverse contents, a plastic box, a stack of lettered cards, the top of a tomato sculpture, a handful of film loops (shown in Figure 2).

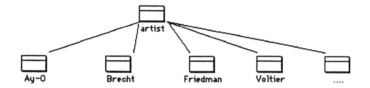

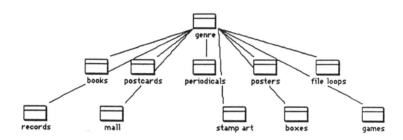

The lettered envelope is selected as shown in Figure 3. One by one, the user can take the monograms of the contributing artists out, placing them wherever they desire on the screen (Figure 4).

So much for objects that are designed to be viewed as stills. But what about motion? Those film loops? Users can select a film loop, and play it.

Interestingly, we do not know for certain which artists contributed each film loop. For this reason, Fluxbase is constructed so that users can name the artist they believe constructed the work. This is especially important when artists themselves use the program. Many are walking repositories of insight and information that can be easily tapped into this informal network. This is a form of electronic scholarship. Moving beyond viewing to participation, George Brecht's *Games & Puzzles* is selected (Figure 5). Opening it reveals assorted marbles, some word puzzles and so on (Figure 6). Again, we can move them around. While movements are presently restricted to a 2-D surface, a greater 3-D illusion will be created by increasing or decreasing the size of the digitized image as the user moves the mouse forward and backward with a depressed command key.

Figure 7 indicates where audio data will be incorporated to extend the range of information. On one side is the program (Figure 7) and on the other a set of cards. And just as it is in the real world, if one person does not clean up a mess, the next person who enters the collection will be faced with a slightly untidy arrangement where the cards were not put away.

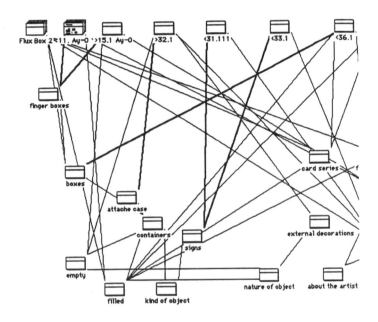

In addition to selecting graphically, users can choose from a textual list as well (Figure 8). Text is also used for the more traditional database aspects. Another feature planned is an option to view "real size" which may be smaller or larger than that presently seen on the screen.

Linking information will be displayed in a network mode; users will select a node for further information such as:

more information about Fluxus
Fluxus lineage

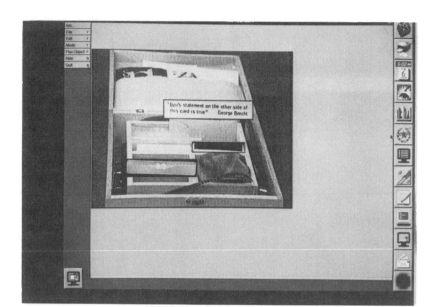

Figure 2.

Figure 3.

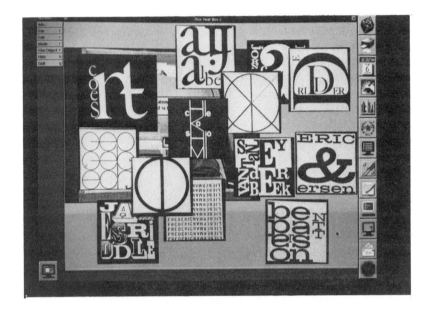

Figure 4.

Figure 5.

alternative educational systems
Black Mountain College
New School of Social Research
artists
Yves Klein
Daniel Spoerri
music
John Cage
religion
Zen Buddhism
formal characteristics of Fluxus (Higgins)
Fluxus methods of community
mail
mall
press, underground
galleries
storefronts
Fluxus progeny
intermedia
correspondence art
performance art
book art

Selecting Hardware and Software Environment

A choice of several environments was available for developing Flux-base: the Macintosh II, the NeXT Computer, and the IBM PS/2. At the time this project began, the most capable IBM system we had available to us was a PS/2 Model 30 with an EGA monitor. This platform was not robust enough to deliver the high-quality graphical display, nor was it fast enough to support the near real-time manipulation necessary. The choice was narrowed to the NeXT Computer and the Macintosh. The NeXT Computer was a new arrival and our programming efforts had been devoted mainly to learning and evaluation. We were interested in gaining experience with the NeXT environment on a larger project, but needed to be sure that there were no overriding advantages favoring the Macintosh. We were also limited to using the resources available at the time, since there was no budget for acquiring additional hardware or software.

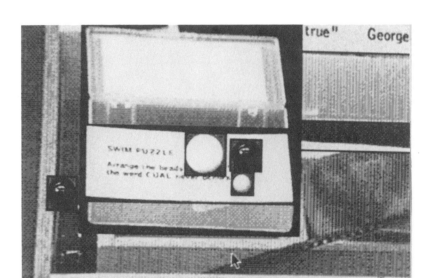

Figure 6.

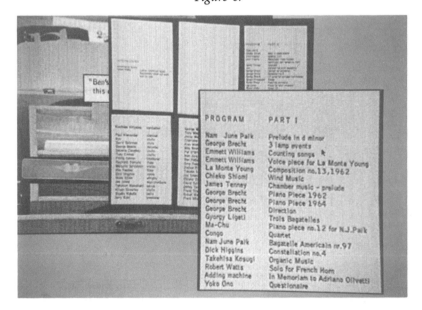

Figure 7.

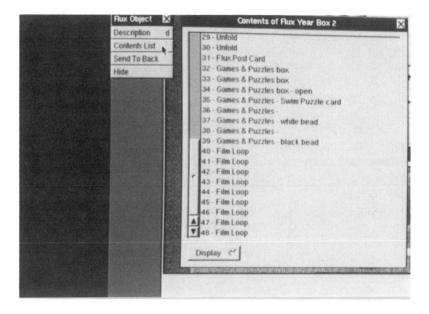

Figure 8.

Hardware Considerations

A high-quality graphics display is obviously required to provide a realistic representation of a visual art object. Although the Macintosh II currently has superior color capabilities, we judged the NeXT's grayscale display adequate for this application because the *Flux Year Box 2* uses predominantly black-and-white tones. Also, the NeXT Computer's standard screen provided a larger area to present and manipulate the contents of the box. Since we planned to store a combination of color images, text, and possibly sound files, disk storage requirements were a concern. NeXT rewritable optical disks stores 256 megabytes, which is sufficient for our prototype. Optical drives for the Macintosh are still expensive, or at least beyond our budget, so it would have been necessary to use the Mac's internal 80 megabyte hard disk drive. Space was insufficient on the Macintosh since we use this computer for a number of other ongoing projects.

Sounds require tools for recording and playback. While the NeXT Computer can record and playback CD quality sound, without external hardware for better analog-to-digital (A/D) conversion, it can only record telephone-quality sound. The Macintosh has no standard hardware for A/D conversion, but we have a third-party device, the Farallon MacRecorder, which allows good recordings at a reasonable cost. Although we did not incorporate audio in the initial prototype, we are including it in the expanded program. The 22 KHz sampling rate of the MacRecorder is sufficient for our needs, so we will probably record audio passages on the Mac, transfer the files to the NeXT, and convert them to a NeXT sound file.

Given that objects are housed in collections at museums across the country, and that the physical movement of objects (such as mail art) was important to the Fluxus community in particular, we wanted a future version of the program to be able to communicate with like programs at other locations. This will require potentially quite sophisticated networking capabilities. The NeXT has a built-in Ethernet port which supports much faster communications than the Macintosh's LocalTalk system. Certainly an Ethernet board could be added to the Macintosh. Indeed, practically all types of hardware could be added to make the systems virtually identical. Ultimately, it was the software environment which influenced our decision and it is to that issue we now turn.

Software Considerations

In Figure 4 is a representative view of the box with its contents strewn around the display. Each of the "monogram cards" in the picture can be dragged around the screen, or put back in the packet from which they came. The desire to treat the computer representations of the art objects in Flux Year Box 2 as separate entities with similar behavior lends itself naturally to implementation with object-oriented methodologies; so does the construction of a graphic user interface. Therefore, our search was focused on software development tools that supported the object-oriented paradigm. On the Macintosh was Object Pascal, HyperCard, and SuperCard. The only practical option on the NeXT Computer was programming in Objective-C using the "objects" provided in the AppKit. This was not as limiting as it might sound since the AppKit provides a great deal of functionality, and support for object-oriented programming techniques is fundamental to the development tools.

HyperCard is probably the most familiar of the Macintosh tools. Its cards, buttons, and message hierarchy support a limited form of object-oriented development. However, we immediately ruled it out because it does not support color, only one card can be open at a time, and it could not treat graphic objects as separate, programmable entities.

SuperCard was more promising; it had those features which Hyper-Card lacked, and a more powerful programming language to match. However, we considered the need for additional flexibility available from a language such as Pascal or C, especially in the areas of networking and managing the manipulation of objects in window area. We did not have access to MacApp, Apple's object-oriented environment for Pascal (and now C++), the NeXT Computer was selected.

The NeXT Computer provides a rich set of software tools to support object-oriented development. Central to the system is the AppKit, a class library which provides most of the typical objects which are used to build an application with a graphic user interface, such as windows, buttons, and menus. Another class, the Bitmap, simplified using digitized images in the program. For future development, we would expect to use the Sound class for storing and playing sounds and the Speaker/Listener which allows communication between applications on local or remote systems. We also anticipate that color will be more important as we expand the kinds of art objects in the program. NeXT has promised that color video hardware will be available for the computer. Because we have used the AppKit objects and Display PostScript in the implementation, few or no program changes should be necessary to use color.

Although we chose to implement Fluxbase on the NeXT Computer, we still used a Macintosh II equipped with a frame capture board to digitize the images and crop them to the desired size. We consider the prototype effort a success and hope to continue development in the NeXT environment. Still, new compilers, class libraries, and integrated environments appear regularly on all platforms and will continue to complicate decisions in the future.

Summary

The Fluxbase prototype has been demonstrated innumerable times over the past six months and received either one of two reactions. Either users say nothing and look as if to say, "Now why would you want to do that?" or they smile, a big, slow, wide smile, and they nod their heads up and down, thinking "Now that is what a computer's for!" To paraphrase a familiar expression, some people see the computer as it is and some people see the computer for what it can be. As users are given more widespread and naturalistic access to works of art—indeed to objects of interest in any field—then knowledge of, understanding about, and sheer pleasure in, that field is increased and enhanced immeasurably.

References

Bronson, A.A. *Evidence of the Avant Garde since 1957* . . . Toronto, Canada: Art Metropole, 1984.
Frank, Peter. "Fluxus in New York," from *lightworks* no. 11/12:29–36.
Hogan, M. *Processing Manual for Incoming Materials to Franklin Furnace Archive* (draft), New York, New York: Franklin Furnace Archive, Inc., 1988.

Appendix A

A project submitted to *Projects Class*, Nova Scotia College of Art and Design, Fall 1969.

A. A group of people (anywhere from five to fifteen) are photographed in the same place and approximately the same position in relation to each other every day at the same hour for two weeks. (No diversion from the conventional group photograph taken for school yearbooks, Knights of Columbus annual picnics, etc.) The people need not wear the same clothes or pose exactly the same way each day, but the immediate impression should be almost identical.

B. These photographs are developed and dated (a record about what one person is wearing each day, or something similar, should be kept each day so that the dates will be accurate); each photograph is then described in writing, in detail, either by the person (or persons) who took the pictures or by someone who was not present at the picturetaking. (Note which case was chosen.)

C. Put the photographs together with the texts in one of the following manners:

   1. Both pictures and texts in chronological order.
   2. Pictures in chronological order, but texts scrambled (they are still dated though).
   3. Texts in chronological order but pictures scrambled (and dated).
   4. Scramble the whole thing in some totally random manner so that sometimes pictures are with their proper texts and sometimes not (still dated), and so that the time sequence is broken entirely: "illustration" and text diverge.

If more than one person is doing the project, each one should take a different last step (and take his own photographs of different groups from the others).

Lucy R. Lippard

ASKEVOLD, DAVID
AIRMAIL
Halifax: Nova Scotia College of Art & Design, 1969?
Postcard, 28×9 cm.

(ASKEVOLD, DAVID, ed.)
Projects Class
Halifax: Nova Scotia College of Art & Design, 1969
Various artists submitted proposals to be completed by the students
at NSCAD, set of 12 cards by 12 artists.
each 17.7×12.6 cm.

AYCOCK, ALICE
Projects and Proposals 1971-1978
Allentown: Muhlenberg College, 1978
60 assorted printed sheets in a black binder,
23.5×28.8 cm.

BALDESSARI, JOHN
Ingres and Other Parables
London: Studio International Publications Ltd., 1972
24 pp., 30.6×27.1 cm.

BALDESSARI, JOHN
Throwing Three Balls in the Air to get a Straight Line
(Best of Thirty-six Attempts)
Milano: Giampaolo Prearo/Galleria Toselli, 1973
14 pp., 33.2×24.3 cm.

BALDESSARI, JOHN
Close Cropped Tales
Buffalo: Albright-Knox Art Gallery, CEPA Gallery and Hallwalls, 1981
84 pp., 17.7×22.5 cm.

III. PROMISE

Virtual Reality Design: A Personal View

Brenda Laurel

IN THE BEGINNING God created the heaven and the earth.

And the earth was without form, and void; and darkness was upon the face of the deep. [Genesis 1:12]

There are many different notions about what virtual reality (VR) is and, consequently, how to go about creating it. A central controversy involves the question of whether virtual worlds and the experiences people may have in them are or are not *designed*. One view conceives of virtual reality as an 'empty space' in which participants can exercise the highest form of self-expression, self-discovery, and self-disclosure. As Meredith Bricken puts it, in virtual reality one can be captain of his or her own ship in an ocean of one's own making. [Bricken, personal communication] Proponents of this view often express emphatic resistance to the notion of designed VR worlds because they would foist the designers' imaginations and points of view onto the participant. This view's holy grail is a fantasy amplifier of the purest form, where a person may quite literally manifest the contents of one's imagination. The empty space calls forth and automagically embodies that which is within us.

Peter Brook, a leading twentieth-century drama theorist and director, describes the theatre as an empty space:

I can take any empty space and call it a bare stage. A man walks across this empty space whilst someone else is watching him, and this is all that is needed for an act of theatre to be engaged. [Brook, 1968]

Note that there is a tree-falling-in-the-forest situation embedded in

95

Brook's idea—there must be someone watching. But a more fundamental point is that an empty space is not theatre until some action occurs in it. Playwrights, directors, actors, designers, and technicians fill the empty space with environments, objects, situations, and characters. These can be very simple or very complex elements, but they constitute the necessary materials from which *action*, the central element of dramatic art, is formulated. The action of a given play is formulated wholly from the potential of the particular dramatic world, including the capabilities of objects, the context of environment and situation, and the traits and predispositions of characters.

Using Designed Spaces

Watch improvisational actors in an empty space. The space is soon populated by characters, words, actions, and real or mimed objects. In the performance of a traditional play, those materials are supplied by the playwright in the script. In interactive or participatory theatre, the audience is able to influence the action to a greater or lesser degree, but what is possible is always constrained by materials that are contributed, before and during the performance, by the author, director, and actors. In other words, the world of a drama is a relatively closed universe. The course of the action and the outcome can be variable, but only within the universe of possibilities created by the elements of environment, situation, and character.

The same is true of computer games. For participants, the 'empty space' is filled with the potential for action that has been provided by the game's designer. For designers and programmers, the empty space is filled with tools (hardware, programming languages, utilities) from which worlds will be constructed, and the nature of those worlds are constrained by the nature of the tools. The world is never formless nor void, but saturated with resources and potentialities. The act is never protean, but always collaborative. All of the arts are conversations between artists and participants, mediated by tools and techniques. Virtual reality promises a special kind of conversation—the next logical step beyond participatory theatre or computer games—in which artists and participants share the role of creator.

There are two problems with the 'empty space' view of virtual reality, and both of them concern autonomy. The first is that there is no known means for disgorging the contents of one's imagination without some sort of tools. Whether the tools are words, paintbrushes, direct-manipulation interfaces, or programming languages hardly matters. The point is that tools restrict what is possible, whether we like it or not.

The second problem is that regardless of the tools available, people are generally not very good at 'making it all up from scratch.' Human creativity works best when there are constraints—like banks of a river—that can shape, channel, and suggest. [May, 1975]

Both of these observations suggest that virtual worlds should, in some sense, be *designed*. By 'designed' I mean that a world and the experiences that one can have in it are consciously shaped. The fact is that by their very nature virtual worlds *are* designed, whether we admit to it or not. The danger of denying the presence of design is that we design unconsciously, by default. By acknowledging design as a necessary element in the creation of virtual realities, we open ourselves up to considerations of form, aesthetics, and art. At the very least, we must address ourselves to designing user-friendly tools for people who wish to create their own virtual worlds and experiences. At most, we must discover ways to design part or all of those worlds, including any 'artificial' characters that may inhabit them, to enable people to have experiences that are powerful, interesting, and pleasurable.

Designed Reality and Role Playing

Each of us probably has a personal notion of what virtual reality can and should be. For me, the closest thing is the experience of acting. I have been an actor for twenty-five years, and it is without a doubt the most resonant, rewarding, exciting activity I know. Acting provides the opportunity to explore oneself, art, and the nature of existence from the perspectives of endlessly varied characters, situations, and worlds. It offers us the educational experience of contexts and issues that we cannot encounter in our everyday lives. When I play a role, I learn with my whole self—body, mind, and soul.

One of the things that people object to in the context of VR is the notion that one must step into the shoes of another 'character' (or a mold provided by the artist) to participate in a virtual world. This objection is founded on the notion that the actor becomes the character. For me, and for most of the actors whose work I admire, the process is just the reverse: one discovers through the character a new version of oneself. This process of discovery and invention is made possible by the materials, form, and structure of the play. It is easy to think of the script as a straitjacket—after all, every word is written down in a conventional play. But actors soon discover that there is endless freedom between, among, and beyond the words as one brings the character to life. [Goldman, 1975]

What one gains from trying on the lives and traits of imaginary characters is what might be described as a cubist view of oneself. What I learned from and experienced through Ophelia, Jenny Diver and even Little Mary Sunshine are things that my own life would never have been able to give me. What I yearn for is the chance to go a step beyond these experiences, in a medium where I can become an active co-creator; not only of the characters' thought processes and physical attributes, but also of their choices and actions within their 'virtual' worlds. I also want everybody else to be able to have such experiences.

Dramatic theory and technique can inform the design of VR experiences in ways that are much broader and more varied than the notion of 'interactive drama' in any conventional sense. How do we do it? Unfortunately, that is a volume in itself.[1] Suffice it to say that we must include the following research topics in our continuing work on virtual reality:

- *Dramatic form, structure, and aesthetics.* Both theatre and film are rich and largely untapped veins of useful theory and techniques. Joseph Bates' work at Carnegie Mellon University (Pittsburgh, PA) on a computational theory of drama and narrative is one of the few examples of ongoing work in this area.
- *Speech and natural language processing* (NLP). NLP has fallen prey to the double bind of high expectations and slow growth, but it is nonetheless a necessary component of a truly robust VR system. Work in this area should be prioritized and supported by those academic, research, and commercial institutions which are serious about creating virtual reality systems.
- *Computer-based characters.* Characters (or 'agents') need not be complex models of human personality; indeed, dramatic characters are effective precisely because they are less complex and therefore more discursive and predictable than human beings. [Laurel, 1990 and Laurel et al, 1990 for theory and examples]

VR is an incredibly exciting notion. For people who read science fiction, play computer games, or hang out in amusement parks, it promises to be the fulfillment of a specific set of fantasies. For folks who have not been a part of the process from the beginning, the potential of VR is probably even more awesome. And in the last year, press and pundits have both nurtured and fed on an image of VR in the popular imagination that promises the 'Ultimate Experience.'

The problem, of course, is that if we do not deliver, and deliver soon, on all the implied and stated promises, VR runs the risk of falling into the same credibility, funding, and profile nightmare as AI (artificial intelligence)—only much more quickly. A more sensible strategy is to back off from the hype and identify the key challenges that lie ahead on the road to VR, and then plan our strategy for research and development so that each incremental step can be viable in its own right. Multimedia, interactive art, interface agents, and computer-based entertainment all provide excellent intermediate platforms for working on some of the central problems in VR.

In the last three years, VR researchers have achieved a quantum leap in the ability to provide sensory immersion. Now it is time to turn our attention to the emotional, cognitive, and aesthetic dimensions of human experience in virtual worlds.

Acknowledgments

I am especially grateful to Bob Jacobson, Associate Director of the new Human Interface Laboratory at the University of Washington in Seattle, for the inspiring conversation that led to this article. I also want to thank Scott Fisher, Michael Naimark, Timothy Leary, Rachel Strickland, Eric Hulteen, and William and Meredith Bricken for their insights.

References

Brook, Peter. *The Empty Space.* New York: Atheneum Publishers, 1968.

Goldman, Michael. *The Actor's Freedom: Toward a Theory of Drama.* New York: The Viking Press, 1975.

Laurel, Brenda, Abbe Don, and Tim Oren. "Issues in Multimedia Interface Design: Media Integration and Interface Agents." *Proceedings of CHI '90,* ACM, April 1990.

Laurel, Brenda. "Interface Agents: Metaphors with Character." In *The Art of Human-Computer Interface Design,* B. Laurel, ed. Reading, MA: Addison-Wesley Publishing Co., 1990.

May, Rollo. *The Courage to Create.* New York: New York: W. W. Norton and Co., 1975.

Interested readers may want to have a look at my dissertation, "Toward the Design of a Computer-Based Interactive Fantasy System," Ohio State University, 1986. A theatre-based theory of human-computer activity and associated design principles and techniques are presented in my forthcoming book, *Computers as Theatre,* Addison-Wesley Publishing Company (early 1991).

Virtual Environments: Personal Simulations & Telepresence

Scott S. Fisher

Media Technology and Simulation
of First-Person Experience

Watch out for a remarkable new process called SENSORAMA! It attempts to engulf the viewer in the stimuli of reality. Viewing of the color stereo film is replete with binaural sound, colors, winds, and vibration. The original scene is recreated with remarkable fidelity. At this time, the system comes closer to duplicating reality than any other system we have seen![1]

For most people, "duplicating reality" is an assumed, if not obvious goal for any contemporary imaging technology. The proof of the 'ideal' picture is not being able to discern object from representation—to be convinced that one is looking at the real thing. At best, this judgment is usually based on a first order evaluation of 'ease of identification'; i.e., realistic pictures should resemble what they represent. But resemblance is only part of the effect. In summing up prevailing theories on realism in images, Perkins comments:

Pictures inform by packaging information in light in essentially the same form that real objects and scenes package it, and the perceiver unwraps that package in essentially the same way.[2]

What is most limited in contemporary media is the literal process involved in 'unwrapping' the image. Evaluation of image realism should also be based on how closely the presentation medium can simulate dynamic, multimodal perception in the real world. A truly informative picture, in addition to merely being an informational surrogate, would duplicate the physicality of confronting the real scene that it is meant to represent. The image would move beyond simple photorealism to immerse the viewer in an interactive, multi-sensory display environment.

Methods to implement and evaluate these interdependent factors contributing to image realism lie in the emerging domain of media technology. Until recently, significant developments in this area have usually been dictated by economics, available technology and, as mentioned, cursory ideas about what types of information are sufficient in image representation. For example, the medium of television, as most experience it, plays to a passive audience. It has little to do with the nominal ability to 'see at a distance' other than in a vicarious sense; it offers only interpretations of remote events as seen through the eyes of others with no capability for viewpoint control or personal exploration. And, although this second-hand information may be better than no information at all, a 'first-person,' interactive point of view can offer added dimensions of experience:

> We obtain raw, direct information in the process of interacting with the situations we encounter. Rarely intensive, direct experience has the advantage of coming through the totality of our internal processes—conscious, unconscious, visceral and mental—and is most completely tested and evaluated by our nature. Processed, digested, abstracted second-hand knowledge is often more generalized and concentrated, but usually affects us only intellectually—lacking the balance and completeness of experienced situations. . . . Although we are existing more and more in the realms of abstract, generalized concepts and principles, our roots are in direct experience on many levels, as is most of our ability to consciously and unconsciously evaluate information.[3]

In the past few decades, changing trends in media technology have begun to yield innovative ways to represent first-person or 'direct experience' through the development of multi-sensory media environments in which the viewer can interact with the information presented as they would in encountering the original scene. A key feature of these display systems (and of more expensive simulation systems) is that the viewer's movements are nonprogrammed; that is, they are free to choose their own path through available information rather than remain restricted to passively watching a 'guided tour.' For these systems to operate effectively, a comprehensive information database must be available to allow the user sufficient points of view. The main objective is to liberate the user enough to move around in a virtual environment, or, on a smaller scale, to viscerally peruse a scene that may be remotely sensed or synthetically generated. In essence, the viewer's access to more than one viewpoint of a given scene allows them to synthesize a strong visual perception; the availability of multiple points of view places an object in context and thereby animates its meaning.

The Evolution of Virtual Environments

Matching visual display technology as closely as possible to human cognitive and sensory capabilities in order to better represent 'direct experience' has been a major objective in the arts, research, and industry for decades. A familiar example is the development of stereoscopic movies in the early 1950s, which created a perception of depth by presenting a slightly different image to each eye of the viewer. In competition with stereo during the same era was Cinerama, which involved three different projectors presenting a wide field of view display to the audience; by extending the size of the projected image, the viewer's peripheral field of view was also engaged. More recently, the Omnimax projection system further expands the panoramic experience by situating the audience under a huge hemispherical dome onto which a high-resolution, predistorted film image is projected; the audience is now almost immersed in a gigantic surrounding image.

In 1962, the "Sensorama" display previously noted was a remarkable attempt at simulating personal experience of several real environments using state of the art media technology. The system was an elegant prototype of an arcade game designed by Morton Heilig, one of the first examples of a multi-sensory simulation environment that provided more than just visual input. When you put your head up to a binocular viewing optics system, you would see a first-person stereo film loop of a motorcycle ride through New York City and with three-dimensional binaural sounds of the city and of the motorcycle moving through it. As you leaned your arms on the handlebar platform built into the prototype and sat in the seat, simulated vibration cues were presented. The prototype also had a fan for wind simulation that worked with a chemical smell bank to blow simulated smells in the viewer's face. As an environmental simulation, the Sensorama display was one of the first steps toward duplicating a viewer's act of confronting a real scene. The user is totally immersed in an information booth designed to imitate the mode of exploration while the scene is imaged simultaneously through several senses.

The idea of sitting *inside* an image has been used in the field of aerospace simulation for many decades to train pilots and astronauts to safely control complex, expensive vehicles through simulated mission environments. Recently, this technology has been adapted for entertainment and educational use. 'Tour of the Universe' in Toronto and 'Star Tours' at Disneyland are among the first entertainment applications of simulation technology and virtual display environments where approximately 40 people sit in a room on top of a motion platform that moves synchronously with a computer-generated and model-based image display of a ride through a simulated universe.

This technology has been moving gradually toward lower cost 'personal simulation' environments in which the viewer is also able to control their own viewpoint or motion through a virtual environment—an important capability missing from the Sensorama prototype. An early example of this is the Aspen Movie Map, done by the M.I.T. (Massachusetts Institute of Technology) Architecture Machine Group in the late 1970s.[4] Imagery of the town of Aspen, Colorado was shot with a special camera system mounted on top of a car, filming down every street and around every corner in town, combined with shots above town from cranes, helicopters and airplanes and also with shots inside buildings. The Movie Map gave the operators the capability of sitting in front of a touch-sensitive display screen and driving through the town of Aspen at their own speed, taking any chosen route by touching the screen, indicating the turns they wanted to make, and which buildings they wanted to enter. In one configuration, this was set up so that the operator was surrounded by front, back, and side-looking camera imagery so that they were completely immersed in a virtual representation of the town.

Conceptual versions of the ultimate sensory-matched virtual environment have been described by science fiction writers for many decades. One concept has been called "telepresence," a technology that would allow remotely situated operators to receive enough sensory feedback to feel like they are really at a remote location and are able to do different kinds of tasks. Arthur Clarke has described 'personalized television safaris' in which the operator could virtually explore remote environments without danger or discomfort. Heinlein's "waldoes" were similar, but were able to exaggerate certain sensory capabilities so that the operator could, for example, control a huge robot. Since 1950, technology has gradually been developed to make telepresence a reality.

Historically, one of the first attempts at developing these telepresence visual systems was done by the Philco Corporation in 1958. With this system an operator could see an image from a remote camera on a CRT mounted on his head in front of his eyes and could control the camera's viewpoint by moving his head.[5] A variation of the head-mounted display concept was done by Ivan Sutherland at M.I.T. in the late 1960s.[6] This helmet-mounted display had a see-through capability so that computer-generated graphics could be viewed superimposed onto the real environment. As the viewer moved around, those objects would appear to be stable within that real environment, and could be manipulated with various input devices that they also developed. Research continues at other laboratories such as NASA Ames in California, the Naval Ocean Systems Center in Hawaii and MITI's Teleexistence Project in Japan. The driving force of these projects is the need to develop improved systems for humans to operate safely and effectively in hazardous environments such as the ocean or outer space.

VIEW: The NASA Ames Virtual Environment Workstation

In the Aerospace Human Factors Research Division of NASA's Ames Research Center, an interactive Virtual Interface Environment Workstation (VIEW) has been developed as a new kind of media-based display and control environment that is closely matched to human sensory and cognitive capabilities. The VIEW system provides a virtual auditory and stereoscopic image surrounding that is responsive to inputs from the operator's position, voice and gestures. As a low-cost multi-purpose simulation device, this variable interface configuration allows an operator to virtually explore a 360-degree synthesized or remotely sensed environment and viscerally interact with its components.[7,8,9,10,11]

The current Virtual Interface Environment Workstation system consists of a wide-angle stereoscopic display unit, glove-like devices for multiple degree-of-freedom tactile input, connected speech recognition technology, gesture tracking devices, 3-D auditory display and speech-synthesis technology, and computer graphic and video image generation equipment.

When combined with magnetic head and limb position tracking technology, the head-coupled display presents visual and auditory imagery that appears to completely surround the user in 3-D space. The gloves provide interactive manipulation of virtual objects in virtual environments that are either synthesized with 3-D computer-generated imagery, or that are remotely sensed by user-controlled, stereoscopic video camera configurations. The computer image system enables high performance, real-time 3-D graphics presentation that is generated at rates up to 30 frames per second as required to update image viewpoints in coordination with head and limb motion. Dual independent, synchronized display channels are implemented to present disparate imagery to each eye of the viewer for true stereoscopic depth cues. For real-time video input of remote environments, two miniature CCD (charge-coupled device) video cameras are used to provide stereoscopic imagery. Development and evaluation of several head-coupled, remote camera platform and prototypes is in progress to determine optimal hardware and control configurations for remotely controlled camera systems. Research efforts also include the development of real-time signal processing technology to combine multiple video sources with computer-generated imagery.

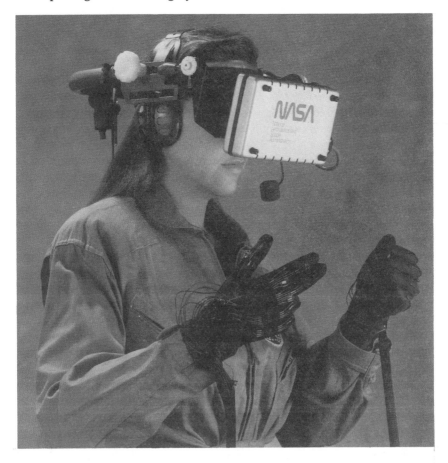

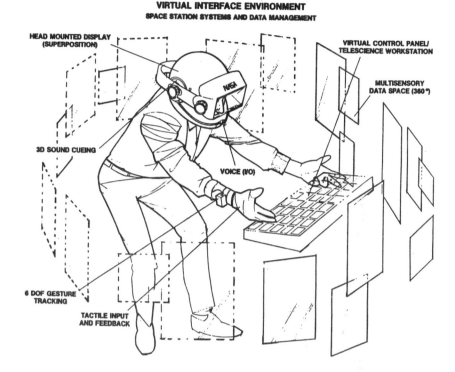

VIRTUAL INTERFACE ENVIRONMENT
SPACE STATION SYSTEMS AND DATA MANAGEMENT

HEAD MOUNTED DISPLAY
(SUPERPOSITION)

VIRTUAL CONTROL PANEL/
TELESCIENCE WORKSTATION

MULTISENSORY
DATA SPACE (360°)

3D SOUND CUEING

VOICE (I/O)

6 DOF GESTURE
TRACKING

TACTILE INPUT
AND FEEDBACK

Virtual Environment Applications

Application areas of the virtual interface environment research at NASA Ames are focused in two main areas, Telepresence and Dataspace:

TELEPRESENCE – The VIEW system is currently used to interact with a simulated telerobotic task environment. The system operator can call up multiple images of the remote task environment that represent viewpoints from free-flying or telerobotmounted camera platforms. Three-dimensional sound cues give distance and direction information for proximate objects and events. Switching to telepresence control mode, the operator's wide-angle, stereoscopic display is directly linked to the telerobot 3-D camera system for precise viewpoint control. Using the tactile input glove technology and speech commands, the operator directly controls the robot arm and dexterous end effector which appear to be spatially correspondent with his own arm.

DATASPACE – Advanced data display and manipulation concepts for information management are being developed with the VIEW system technology. Current efforts include use of the system to create a display environment in which data manipulation and system monitoring tasks are organized in virtual display space around the operator. Through speech and gesture interaction with the virtual display, the operator can rapidly call up or delete information windows and reposition them in 3-D space. Three-dimensional sound cues and speech-synthesis technologies are used to enhance the operator's overall situational awareness of the virtual data environment. The system also has the capability to display reconfigurable, virtual control panels that respond to glove-like tactile input devices worn by the operator.

Personal Simulation:
Architecture, Medicine, Entertainment

In addition to remote manipulation and information management tasks, the VIEW system also may be a viable interface for several commercial applications. So far, the system has been used to develop simple architectural simulations that enable the operator to design a very small 3-D model of a space, and then, using a glove gesture, scale the model to life size. This would allow the architect/operator to "walk" around in the designed space. Seismic data, molecular models, and meteorological data are other examples of multi-dimensional data that may be better understood through representation and interaction in a virtual environment.

Another virtual environment scenario in progress involves the development of a surgical simulator for medical students and plastic surgeons that could be used much as a flight simulator is used to train jet pilots. Where the pilot can actually explore situations that would be dangerous to encounter in the real world, surgeons can use a simulated "electronic cadaver" to do pre-operation planning and patient analysis. The system is also set up in such a way that surgical students can look through the eyes of a senior surgeon and see a first-person view of the way he or she is doing a particular procedure. As illustrated in the following figure, the surgeon can be surrounded with the kinds of information windows that are typically seen in an operating room in the form of monitors displaying life-support systems status information and X-rays.

Entertainment and educational applications of this technology could be developed through this ability to simulate a wide range of real or fantasy environments with almost infinite possibilities of scale and extent. The user can be immersed in a 360-degree fantasy adventure game as easily as he or she can viscerally explore a virtual 3-D model of the solar system or use a three-dimensional paint system to create virtual environments for others to explore.

Tele-Collaboration Through Virtual Presence

A major near-term goal for the Virtual Environment Workstation Project is to connect at least two of the current prototype interface systems to a common virtual environment database. The two users will participate and interact in a shared virtual environment but each will view it from their relative, spatially disparate viewpoint. The objective is to provide a collaborative workspace in which remotely located participants can virtually interact with some of the nuances of face-to-face meetings while also having access to their personal dataspace facilities. This could enable valuable interaction between scientists collaborating from different locations across the country or even between astronauts on a space station and research labs on Earth. With full-body tracking capability, it will also be possible for each user to be represented in this space by his or her own life-size virtual representation in any chosen form—a kind of electronic persona. For interactive theater or interactive fantasy applications, these virtual forms might range from fantasy figures to inanimate objects or from different figures to different people. Developing telecommunication networks will be eventually configured with virtual environment servers for remote-dialing interactions with other virtually present users.

Although the current prototype of the Virtual Environment Workstation has been developed primarily to be used as a laboratory facility, the components have been designed to be easily replicable for relatively low cost. As the processing power and graphics frame rate on microcomputers quickly increases, portable and personal virtual environment systems will also become readily available. The possibilities of virtual realities, it appears, are as limitless as the possibilities of reality. It provides a human interface that disappears—a doorway to other worlds.

Notes

1. Lipton, L. July 1964. "Sensorama," *Popular Photography.*
2. Perkins, D.N. 1979. "Pictures and the Real Thing," Project Zero, Harvard University, Cambridge, Massachusetts.

3. Bender, T. 1973. Environmental Design Primer.

4. Lippman, Andrew. 1980. "MovieMaps: An Application of the Optical Videodisc to Computer Graphics," *Computer Graphics.* 14:3.

5. Comeau, C. and Bryan J. 1961. "Headsight Television System Provides Remote Surveillance," *Electronics.* Nov. 10, 1961: 86–90.

6. Sutherland, I.E. 1968. "Head-Mounted Three-Dimensional Display," *Proceedings of the Fall Joint Computer Conference,* 757–764.

7. Fisher, Scott S. 1986. "Telepresence Master Glove Controller for Dexterous Robotic End-Effectors", *Advances in Intelligent Robotics Systems.* D.P. Casasent, Editor, Proc. SPIE 726, 1986.

8. Fisher, S.S., McGreevy, M., Humphries, J., Robinett, W., 1986. "Virtual Environment Display System," ACM 1986 Workshop on 3-D Interactive Graphics, Chapel Hill, North Carolina. October 23–24, 1986.

9. Fisher, S.S., Wenzel, E.M., Coler, C., McGreevy, M.W. 1988. "Virtual Interface Environment Workstations," *Proceedings of the Human Factors Society 32nd Annual Meeting* (Oct. 24–28, 1988, Anaheim, California).

10. Wenzel, E.M., Wightman, F.L., Foster, S.H., 1988. "A Virtual Display System for Conveying Three-Dimensional Acoustic Information," *Proceedings of the Human Factors Society 32nd Annual Meeting* (Oct. 24–28, 1988, Anaheim, California).

11. Foley, James D. 1987. "Interfaces for Advanced Computing." *Scientific American.* 257, no. 4: 126–135.

Simulated World as Classroom: The Potential For Designed Learning within Virtual Environments

David C. Traub

This chapter explores the use of computer-generated "virtual reality" environments as an ideal milieu for learning. The context for this exploration is the notion of "Knowledge as Design,"[1] by David Perkins from Harvard University. Perkins defines design as "the human endeavor of shaping objects to purposes"[2] with knowledge as the object. In this learning model an intended instruction is broken into a series of four discrete informational constructs (knowledge, representation, retrieval and construction)[3] that together comprise the greater cognitive activities associated with learning. By designing a learning experience according to this cognitive template, it is possible to optimize the potential for creating a comprehensive and effective learning experience for any body of knowledge.

The rapidly evolving "virtual reality" technologies—those that enable the design of simulated 3-D computer-graphic realities within which a user may directly explore in the "first person"[4]— provide, in theory, an optimal interactive technology for the application of Perkins' learning design methodology to all forms of knowledge. While these technologies are not quite evolved to the point of enabling complex, real-time and dynamic interactions with realistic, simulated characters, converging computer and AI (artificial intelligence) technologies supporting virtual reality are moving in this direction.

This chapter briefly describes Perkins' learning template. Virtual reality is defined and an exemplary example of an imagined virtual reality learning experience, in this case an exploration of the use of virtual reality in the teaching of history is described. Finally, caveats concerning the likelihood of virtual reality actually finding its way into institutional learning environments for quite some time are presented. Its potential as an ultimate learning tool is unlikely to be implemented where it is most needed—in addressing the U.S.'s educational crisis. In addition to cost factors, it is typical that new technologies are first channeled to institutions such as the military, business and entertainment industries that American society deems more important.

Introduction

The evolving optical formats—videodisc, CD-I and CD-ROM—are each being positioned for adaptation by educators wishing to provide students with access to information-rich multimedia databases. Compared with previous computer-based systems, these optical media are unique for several reasons. They have full-motion video capabilities which engage the user in an experience that may approach the familiarity of television. They allow students to explore materials and lessons at their own pace and inclination. Compared to conventional educational strategies such as lecture, drilling and testing, these media indicate entirely new outcomes for shared responsibility and effectiveness in the acquisition and integration of knowledge.

Yet, these technologies are but one component to an evolving mix of "hard" (machine-intervention), "soft" (human-intervention), and "combination" (machine-assisted human interventions) technologies which are converging to reconfigure the institutional, corporate and domestic learning environments of the 1990s. For example, the documented success of "human-based" learning technologies such as "peer-peer" collaborative learning is bringing new respect to the student as a partner in his or her own education. The exponential success of telecom-based distance learning and its online "master teacher-student" paradigm is firmly establishing the immense value that one-on-one rapport and mentorship brings to any learning context.

What is evolving are an increasing variety of human and technology-based tools for learning vying for attention and adaptation. Each represents one or several didactic assets that can be substantiated as viable to the educational process, in some cases in collaboration with other tools or processes. The question arises: how is the proper instructional mix chosen? By what ultimate and affordable combination of technologies and techniques might an institution optimize its mission of teaching? How can we optimize our chances to teach students in a manner that fosters the long-term integration?

Knowledge As Design

David Perkins, co-director of the Harvard Graduate School of Education's Project Zero, has sculpted a unique theory of learning and understanding based on the application of design methodologies to the acquisition of knowledge. In this methodology, a specific learning intention is broken into the four categories of understanding that he calls an " 'access framework' for the analysis and design of instructional interventions."[5] In this framework, an educational event is broken up into four distinctive cognitive constructs identified as "(1) knowledge and know-how, (2) representation, (3) retrieval and (4) construction."[6] Each is then broken into further sub-species of questions that complete a taxonomy by which all components of a potential learning event might be first analyzed, and then designed.

Perkins' template provides a logical means for considering each of the above-described technological and methodological means for teaching as a function of each unique learning experience. For example, when considering the teaching of history, one might first consider the application of Perkins' construct of knowledge. Broken up into "content, problem-solving, epistemic knowledge and inquiry,"[7] a designer might consider that a lesson must consider the acquisition of facts regarding a particular period of time, the application of these facts within a problem-solving operation, the application of historic justification, and further inquiry into the validity of a historic figure's actions.

Applying this analysis to an appropriation of technologies, Perkins' model might suggest:

- the use of books and videos for the acquisition of concepts and data,
- the use of collaborative simulations games to encourage student-based problem-solving,
- the writing of essays to justify the actions the student engages in simulating historic characters, and
- the use of teacher-led discussions to explore fundamental assumptions the original historic characters may have made when they engaged in their original activities.

The teacher would continue on a similar bent of analysis and design along the axis of the three other cognitive constructs to complete the development of a lesson that might optimally teach.

Yet while Perkins' methodology provides a strong tool for effectively designing a lesson across a variety of delivery systems, its power is theoretically most evident in its application to computer-simulated environments that are readily malleable to the dictates of a design, instead of the reverse. It should certainly be easier to create the computer-generated simulated rendering of a complex historic event such as the Civil War (or the decline of the dinosaur) than it might be, for example, to use existing footage. Certainly the ability to accurately simulate historic phenomenon could be tailored to comply with the purposes of an instructional design although such apparently "truth-rendering" representation will incite questions of perspective and ethics.[8]

Evolving virtual reality technologies enable first person user interaction with simulated realities of a historic (or other) nature. They provide favorable environments for the construction of design-based learning experiences tailored by the specific needs of a particular education purpose. However, what is virtual reality and how can it be used in an educational context?

The Technology

Piaget once said that the ultimate path to learning is through life itself. Since reading this quote, I have sought the ultimate learning environment for exploring a variety of learning situations. My goal is a simulation-based environment that minimizes interface, or the distance between user and interactive content, while maximizing the user's ability to control discovery within the context of an external pedagogical intention. I have continually pursued the experience of the "Holodeck."[9]

Of late there is a growing convergence of three technologies that might soon enable such a simulation-based environment:

- Artificial Intelligence for the creation of narrative rule-based interpolation of scripted narrative behaviors, allowing audience input in the construction and maintenance of "filmic" or other visually represented continuities;
- 3-D computer-generated projection systems such as Autodesk's Cyberspace which enables users to don a sensor-laden head-mounted display system and access computer-graphic generated realities; and
- Digital signal processing (DSP)-based video projection systems such as Vivid Effects Mandala system which allow the likeness of a user to be integrated into a computer-generated synthetic reality whereby the user witnesses his or her own image as an integral component of that synthetic reality.

Together with other developing virtual reality interface clothing, these systems combine to create the marriage of two evolving concepts, the concepts of "virtual reality" and "interactive cinema." "Virtual reality" is the term given a family of emerging videocomputing systems such as the ones described above which facilitate the creation of synthetic computer graphic "virtual" environments in which one may explore in the first person with the aid of head-mounted display, video superimposition, and/or other means of body tracking interface. "Interactive cinema" describes a cinematic model in which the audience, assuming the role of first- or second-person, influences the unfolding outcome of a story. The potential for interactive cinema continues to increase with the evolution of rule-based control systems which continuously reconfigure the continuity of a story drawn from a database of parsed cinematic components (shots and sequences), according to user input and pre-programmed cinematic logic.

Taken together, these technologies could theoretically accommodate the first- or second-person experiences within the context of some hypothetical interactive theater complex, an "interactive virtual reality" allowing the user to design simulated learning environments.

History As A Virtual Design

At a recent Intertainment Conference, novelist Isaac Asimov said that our brains, "by far the most complex matter in the universe, are built for amusement, and learning is the optimal path to amusement."[10] The phrase "history as design" might aptly describe one learning experience intended for experience-hungry users—one of many programs included in a system that comes with a variety of simulations "programs." It is a situation that will let the user "design" simulated dynamic historic microsystems[11] capable of orchestrating a variety of historic scenarios the user might then experience first-hand.

It will be an experience that will then allow the "observation" of these simulated occurences under a variety of internally and externally-generated stimulus, or even "participate" in the first person. In so doing the user will either principally or vicariously gain access to the positive—and negative—dynamics of this complex interaction.

Providing a user with the ability to construct, and therefore appreciate, the dynamic nature of a historic context gives the tools for pondering its complexity. To offer the user the ability to project this formulation over time might enable them to project the specific historic development over time or even anticipate how else it might have been resolved.

An option to interact dynamically with this model is an opportunity for the user to develop experiential access to behaviors arising from this interaction.

The "History Room"

The educational purpose of this hypothetical simulated virtual reality "History Room" is to make available a casually-accessed educational environment permitting users to design, construct and interact with dynamic historic microsystems. The end result would be to develop a potentially better "general" understanding of the inherent complexities in the experience of a specific historical period or event, as well as channeling this new insight into an understanding of the user's own place in the historical continuum.

Access Framework

There are numerous ways a simulated "virtual reality" environment can be used to help teach the content and skills described above, or other systems of knowledge. These pathways are explained using David Perkins' framework for considering understanding as knowledge, representation, retrieval and construction.[12]

Knowledge

Content is assimilated by witnessing the projection of the historical, physical attributes of the scene as might be described by historians. For example, the physical conditions of a certain conflict can be articulated as a function of procedures, place, time, physical features, activity, participants, and an appropriate role could be imagined.[13]

Problem-Solving is manifested by the user's ability to construct a historical situation. He or she can witness conflicts that might evolve from this construction, then intervene so it might serve to undermine the instigating conflict.

Epistemic knowledge is realized while the user witnesses both the construction of these simulated events and their pursuant interactions. Such witnessing provides knowledge not only into how our understanding of these events is constructed, but also into how we use this historical knowledge to justify nationalistic behaviors.

Inquiry, the fourth of the "knowledge series," is facilitated as the user purposely stretches boundaries of the historic dynamic, exploring the interactions that occur, for example, if he or she promotes a bellicose behavior on the part of one of the players. Inquiry might also be facilitated by building a component of randomness into the progression towards denouement, thereby enabling the user to witness a variety of new interactions not previously anticipated.

Representation

As with general content, *facts* about the event become clear to the user as particular known behaviors are initiated and revealed in action. At the same time, the user can use the system to represent *facts* to others as a function of the constructions used, rather than having the "intelligence" of the system reveal them to the user.

The History Room also provides a unique means of presenting information to both users and their audiences by using the following:(1) a specific time in history as a *conceptual network* through which a variety of behaviors can be witnessed, and (2) as a *conceptual anchor* upon which specific concepts or ideas can be based. For example, one can use specific characters, in all their intrapersonal complexity, to act as the *conceptual network* upon which to reveal insights, or as the *conceptual anchor* upon which to string relevant attributes and behaviors.

Modeling is by far the most significant use of the History Room as a "concrete, coherent and conceptual" means of representation. According to Perkins, "research on memory has demonstrably shown that organization, imagery, and meaningfulness foster memory . . . models provide visualizations and dramatizations, both providing imagery."[14] The ability to simulate virtual environments which the user might enter and participate is certainly a powerful use of modeling, one bringing the user even closer to the content, as it is in real life. The ability of a model to "make something understandable by showing, manifesting, or displaying its characteristics"[15] makes it an ideal means of teaching complex historical issues, particularly those emeshed within several significant axes. Most important, the capability of this particular "interactive virtual" model to:

1. produce a most interesting activity,
2. permit decision-making,
3. maximize informative feedback,
4. potentially collaborate interactions;
5. allow the user to develop their own problems along a range of difficulties;
6. engage a user in these activities without the onus of surveillance (at the user's discretion); and finally

7. promote an experience that is most certainly going to be 'fun'[16]

will undoubtedly make this educational model a most popular environment for learning.

Most of the other aspects of modeling can be hardly realized by
this model, such as multiple representations from different directions,
the modeling of target performances, the use of contrasting representations to arrive at a fresh insight, etc.

Retrieval

Using the simulated model yields a myriad of retrieval options. Not
only does the visual model provide an excellent means of helping an
audience to retain knowledge gained from the experience through an
enhanced identification with one or several of the simulated characters,
but the system's ability to assist the user in perpetually "reconfigur-
ing" various situations will enable this user to conceive, design, create
and explore a vast variety of social constructs, each potentially representing some unique attribute of human dynamics. In other words, user-
generated history systems will present many with the opportunities
to formulate a variety of insights to which they might not have had
previous access.

By the same token, the myriad of random or otherwise unexpected
behavioral actions resulting from various interactions among the
characters will most certainly bring a variety of insights and questions
to the surface. Perhaps the user will then feel encouraged, to again
reconfigure this scenario with the possibility of finding yet more significant issues.

Construction

While there is ample opportunity for *elaborative processing*[17] in this virtual world—a learning paradigm by which a user has access to a variety of topical or accessible knowledge, the greatest beauty of the History
Room is its ability to facilitate a *working through* approach to solving
problems. This approach takes the form of problem-finding, while
problem-solving, in contrast, provides a more thorough and flexible
mindset when directed in efforts to understand and resolve a problem.
The ability to design, construct and interact with simulated human constructs leads to an ideal path for anticipating, recognizing, understanding and finally combining inter- and intrapersonal knowledge into real-
life contexts.

Theatric Models For Learning Environment

In this environment, historic learning will occur within some self-contained virtual cubicle. The user might proceed as follows: (1) the user enters the cube, proceeds to the touchscreen interface and begins to choose among several historical periods and characters, or even create their own from options such as period, class, significance, occupation, historic dynamics (i.e., the menu might offer a variety of character options describing increasingly complex characterizations); (2) then the user dons the head-mounted display, moving to the center of the room; (3) noting a "virtual" menu that further describes behavioral options, the user clicks on an imaginary start button. The games begin as the historic events unfold within the cubicle and continue as the user faces periodic options to effect the progression.

Instructional Problem and Arguments

There are several arguments for the treatment of simulated conflicts within the context of machine-facilitated interventions. One is the challenge of creating a simulation that the user will readily accept and use, despite current limitations in resolution and the awkward dramatic continuities put forth by today's mediating computers. An ultimate hope for such a system is to give the user sufficient first-person identification in order to explore a reality as if it were real, thereby increasing the potential for long-term learning.

Another problem is the notion of facilitating a technological intervention in the realm of education that might challenge the designer's ability to maintain a pedagogical intention within the context of a user's ability to fashion his or her own experience. Most certainly this latter consideration poses ethical and applications-oriented issues that must be confronted and resolved to the satisfaction of some greater societal moral telos.

Conclusion

For now, it is probably still fantasy to imagine the hypothetical "interactive virtual environment" described in this chapter. Yet, each of the component technologies required to make the vision possible are now thriving beyond prototype and inching towards the market. It seems to be only a matter of time before they will be integrated within single solutions that will be moving in the same direction to market. I toast this certain future with the firm knowledge that there must be positive benefits, in conjunction with, and in support of human interactions, derived from these systems—beyond the military posturing, industrial manufacture and the corporate communications which typically precede the application of new technologies to education. I applaud the efforts of anyone who might use and develop virtual reality technologies with the intention of delivering some pedagogical benefit to a rapidly evolving world culture busily speeding to a technocratic twenty-first century.

Notes

1. Perkins, David N. 1986. *Knowledge As Design.* Lawrence, Erblaum Associates, Publishers.

2. Ibid.

3. Perkins, David N. Handouts for "Knowledge as Design," H-440, Harvard Graduate School of Education, Spring 1990.

4. Laurel, Brenda. *A Taxonomy Of Interactive Movies.* New Media New, (winter 89): 6.

5. Perkins, David N. *Knowledge as Design.* p. 2.

6. Ibid.

7. Ibid.

8. The ethical considerations of simulation, and particularly, the use of virtual reality simulation as an educational media, shall become one of the most significant ethical debates of the 1990s.

9. The Holodeck simulation is a fictional technology borrowed from the television show *Star Trek: The Next Generation* that describes a capacity to simulate virtual worlds that users can explore in the first person as if they were real.

10. Intertainment, '89, New York (keynote speaker).

11. Bronfenbrenner, Urie. "Toward an Experimental Ecology of Human Development." *American Psychologist,* (July 1977): 514. Bronfenbrenner defines a "microsystem" as "the complex of relations between the developing person and environment in an immediate setting containing that person (e.g., home, school, workplace, etc)." While I am positing the use of this environment for the development of simulated historic constructs, I could easily see it applied to other dynamic microsystems, for example those that might take place within other educational constructs such as the understanding of mathematical or scientific concepts.

12. Perkins Handout. Ibid.

13. Bronfenbrenner (page 514) provides examples of some of these characteristics in a definition of the elements setting: "the factors of place, time, physical features, activity, participant, and role."

14. Perkins, David N. *Knowledge As Design*, p.20.
15. Ibid p.126.
16. Ibid p.116.
17. David Perkins Handouts.

Directory
of Companies and Individuals

John Ahrens
Department of Philosophy
University of Hartford
West Hartford, Connecticut

Joel Peter Anderson
NCR Comten
St. Paul, Minnesota

Steven Aukstakalnis
Human Interface Technology Lab
University of Washington
Seattle, WA

John Perry Barlow
Pinedale, Wyoming

Tom Barett
Electronic Data Systems
Richardson, TX

Michael Benedikt
School of Architecture
The University of Texas at Austin

Steve Bingham
Alias
Toronto, Ontario, Canada

Jeffrey Bonar
Guidance Technologies, Inc.
Pittsburgh, Pennsylvania

Meredith Bricken
Human Interface Technology Lab
University of Washington
Seattle, WA

Bradley Brilliant and Kee Hinckley
Alphalpha Software, Inc.
Arlington, MA

Daniel Browning
Autodesk Inc.,
Sausalito, CA

M. Gordon Brown
College of Environmental Design
University of Colorado at Boulder
Boulder, CO

Glorianna Davenport
MIT Media Lab
20 Ames Street
Cambridge, MA 02139

Chris Dede
Advanced Knowledge Transfer Project
University of Houston—Clear Lake
Houston, TX

Kenneth Lee Diamond, Ph.D.
Kingsboro Psychiatric Center
Brooklyn, NY

Susan Eldred
Thomas J. Watson Research Center
IBM
Yorktown Heights, NY 10598

Kim Fairchild
Microelectronics and Computer Technology Corporation
Austin, TX

F. Randall Farmer
Xanadu Operating Company
Palo Alto, CA

Gary Foltz
Autodesk, Inc.
Sausalito, CA

Brian Gaines
Knowledge Science Institute
University of Calgary
Calgary, Alberta, Canada

Philip Galanter
Advanced Technology Group
Northwestern University—ACNS
Evanston, IL

James C. Goodlett, Jr.
College of Architecture
Texas Tech University
Lubbock, TX

Eric Gullichsen
Sense8
1001 Brideway
477
Sausalito, CA 94965

Michael Heim
Department of Philosophy
California State University
Long Beach, CA

Joseph Henderson, M.D.
Interactive Media Laboratory
Dartmouth College
Hanover, New Hampshire 03756

Ron Hess
Interactive Multimedia Group
Cornell University
New York, NY

Roland Hjerppe
Department of Computer and Information Science
Linkoping University
Linkoping, Sweden

Robert E. Horn
The Lexington Institute
Lexington, MA

Craig Hubley
Craig Hubley & Associates
Toronto, Ontario, Canada

Joseph Hunt
Somerville, MA

Robert Jacobson
Human Interface Technology Laboratory
University of Washington
Seattle, WA

Wendy Kellogg
IBM T.J. Watson Research Center
Yorktown, NY

Myron Krueger
Artificial Reality Corporation
55 Edith Road
Vernon, CT 06066

Jaron Lanier
VPL
656 Bear Island Road
Suite 304
Redwood City, CA 94063

Brenda Laurel
Interactivist
Los Gatos, CA

Paul Levinson
Connected Education, Inc.
Bronx, NY

C. Michael Lewis
Department of Information Science
University of Pittsburgh
Pittsburgh, PA

Michael Liebhold
Manager of Media Tools & Applications
Advanced Technology Group
Apple Computer, Inc.
20525 Mariani
Cupertino, CA

Tim McFadden
Altos Computer Systems
San Jose, CA

Michael McGreevy
NASA Ames Research Center
Aerospace Human Factors Research Division
Moffett Field, CA 94035

Aidan McManus
Technology Strategy
American Express Company
New York, NY

Steve O'Connell
Advanced Technology Group
American Express Travel Related Services
Phoenix, AZ

Geoffrey Miller
Department of Psychology
Stanford University
Stanford, CA

J. Michael Moshell
Institute for Simulation and Training
University of Central Florida
Orlando, FL

Marcos Novak
School of Architecture
The University of Texas at Austin
Austin, TX

R. Michael O'Bannon
Georgia Tech Research Institute
Georgia Institute of Technology
Atlanta, GA

Matt Perez
Sun Microsystems
2550 Garcia Avenue
Mountain View, CA 94043

Robert Perl
College of Architecture
Texas Tech University
Lubbock, TX

Rita Pizzi
Department of Information Sciences
University of Milan
Milan, Italy

David Porush
School of Humanities and Social Sciences
Rensselaer Polytechnic
Troy, NY

Steve Pruitt
Texas Instruments
Allen, TX

Vernon Reed
Elektrum
Austin, TX

Mark Spitzglas
College of Architecture
Texas Tech University
Lubbock, TX

Michael Spring
Department of Information Science
727 LIS University of Pittsburgh
Pittsburgh, PA 15260

Natalie Stenger
MIT Center for Advanced Visual Studies
Cambridge, MA

Rory Stuart
NYNEX Artificial Intelligence Lab
White Plains, NY

David Temkin
Institute for Research and Information in Scholarship
Brown University
Providence, RI

Harry Tennant
Information and Knowledge Delivery Branch
Texas Instruments
Dallas, TX

Wes Thomas
Mondo 2000
606 5th Avenue
East Northport
New York, NY 11731

David Traub
Center Point Communications
434 South 1st St.
San Jose, CA 95113

Randal Walser
AutoDesk, Inc.
2320 Marinship Way
Sausalito, CA 94965

Alan Wexelblat
Bull NH Worldwide Information Systems
Billerica, MA

David Zeltzer
MIT Media Lab
MX E 15-231
20 Ames Street
Cambridge, MA 02139

Recommended Readings

Barlow, John Perry, "Being in Nothingness," *Mondo 2000*, (Summer 1990), pp. 34–43.

Barlow, John Perry, "Life in the Data Cloud," *Mondo 2000*, (Summer 1990), pp. 44–51.

Beck, Stephen. "Virtual Light & Cybervideo," *Mondo 2000*, (Summer 1990), 64–65.

Bodisco, Arthur, "Sense8 Plans Affordable VR Now," *Mondo 2000*, 54.

Bricken, William. "Cyberspace 1999," *Mondo 2000*, 56–75.

Brooks, F.P. "Grasping Reality Through Illusion: Interactive Graphics Serving Science." ACM SIGCHI.

Caruso, Denise, "Virtual Reality, Get Real," *Media Letter*, August 1990, Vol. 1, No. 3.

Comeau, C., and Bryan, J. "Headsight Television Systems Provides Remote Surveillance," *Electronics*, Nov. 10, 1961, 86–90.

Crouch, D.B., "A Pictorial Representation of Data in an Information Retrieval Environment," *1987 Workshop on Visual Languages*, August 19–21, 1987, Tryck-Center, Linkoping, Sweden: pp. 177–187.

Ditlea, Steve, "Inside Virtual Reality," *PC/Computing*, Summer 1989, pp. 91–101.

Englebart, D.C., R.W. Watson, and J.C. Norton. "The Augmented Knowledge Workshop," *Proceedings National Computer Conference*, 1973, p. 921.

Farmer, F.R., "Cyberspace: Getting There From Here," *Journal of Computer Game Design*. October 1988.

Fisher, Scott and M. McGreevy, M. Humphries, J. Robinett. Virtual Environment Display System, ACM 1986 Workshop on 3-D Interactive Graphics, Chapel Hill, North Carolina, October 23–24, 1986.

Fisher, Scott, E.M. Wenzel, C. Coler, M. McGreevy. "Virtual Interface Environment Workstations," Proceedings of the Human Factors Society 32nd Annual Meeting (October 24–28, 1988, Anaheim, CA).

Fisher, Scott and Jane Tazelaar. "Living in a Virtual World," Byte, July, 1990, pp. 215–221.

Foley, James D. "Interfaces for Advanced Computing," Scientific American, 257, no. 4: 126–135.

Friedhoff, Richard and William Benzon. Visualization: The Second Computer Revolution, New York: Harry N. Abrams, Inc., 1990.

Gibson, William. Neuromancer. New York: Ace Books, 1984.

Goldstein, Harry, "Virtual Reality," Utne Reader, March/April 1990, pp. 41–42.

Henderson, J. "Cluster Analysis and Rotating 3-D Scatter Plots to Explore and Link a Multimedia Database," Proceedings 13th Symposium on Computer Applications in Medical Care, IEEE, Washington, D.C. 392–398, 1989.

Kelly, K. "Virtual Reality: An Interview with Jaron Lanier." Whole Earth Review, No. 64, pp. 108–109, 1989.

Krueger, Myron. Artificial Reality, Addison-Wesley, 1990.

Larish, John. Understanding Electronic Photography, Summit, PA: TAB Professional, 1990.

Laurel, Brenda. Computers as Theatre, Addison-Wesley, 1991.

Laurel, Brenda, Abbe Don, and Tim Oren. "Issues in Multimedia Interface Design: Media Integration and Interface Agents." Proceedings of CHI '90, ACM, April 1990.

Laurel, Brenda. "On Dramatic Interaction," Verbum, 3.3 pp. 6–7, 1989.

Laurel, Brenda. The Art of Human-Computer Interface Design, Addison-Wesley, 1990.

Laurel, Brenda. *Toward the Design of a Computer-Based Interactive Fantasy System*, Dissertation, Ohio State University, 1986.

Levy, Steven. "Out on a Sim," *Macworld*, April, 1990, pp. 51–53.

Lewis, M.D., "Metaphor in Visualization," Working Paper, Department of Information Science, University of Pittsburgh, PA, 1989.

Lewis, Peter. "Put on Your Data Glove and Goggles and Step Inside," *The New York Times*, Sunday, May 20, 1990, p. 8.

McCormick, B., T. DeFanti, and M. Brown, "Visualization in Scientific Computing," *Computer Graphics*, Vol. 21, no. 6 November 1987, New York: ACM SIGGRAPH.

Nash, Jim. "Bridging the Real and Unreal," *Computerworld*, March 12, 1990, p. 20.

Rheingold, Howard. "Teledildonics," *Mondo 2000*, (Summer 1990), 52–54.

Rogers, Michael. "Now, 'Artificial Reality,' " *Newsweek*, February 9, 1987, pp. 56–57.

Saffo, Paul, "Virtual Reality is Almost Real," *Personal Computing*, June 29, 1990, pp. 99–102.

Scheinin, Richard, "The Artificial Realist," *San Jose Mercury News*, January 29, 1990, p. 1–2.

Smith, R.B., "The Alternative Reality Kit: An Animated Environment for Creating Interactive Simulations," Proceedings of the 1986 IEEE Computer Society Workshop on Visual Languages, June 25–27, 1986, Dallas, Texas, pp. 99–196.

Stratton, Bob. "ImagineNation 'Virtual Reality' for Entertainment," *Mondo 2000*, 63.

Sutherland, I.E. "Headmounted Three Dimensional Display," Proceedings of the Fall Joint Computer Conference, 1968, 757–764.

Thomas, Wes. "Hyperwebs," *Mondo 2000*, (Summer 1990), 68–69.

Thorpe, J.A. "The new technology of large scale simulator networking: implications for mastering the art of warfighting." Ninth Interservice Industry Training Systems Conference, 1987.

Todd, Daniel, "Autodesk: A Success Story," *Information Week*, July 23, 1990.

Walser, R. "Doing it Directly, The Experiential Development of Cyberspaces." Forthcoming in *Proceedings 1990 SPIE/SPSE Symposium on Electronic Imaging Science & Technology*, Santa Clara, CA.

Contributors

Scott S. Fisher attended the Massachusetts Institute of Technology where he held a research fellowship at the Center for Advanced Visual Studies from 1974 to 1976 and was a member of the Architecture Machine Group from 1978 to 1982. There he participated in development of the Aspen Movie Map surrogate travel videodisc project and several stereoscopic display systems for teleconferencing and telepresence applications. He received an M.S. in Media Technology from MIT in 1981. His research interests focus primarily in stereoscopic imaging technologies, interactive display environments and the development of media technology for representing "first-person" sensory experience. From 1985 to 1990, he was founder and Director of the Virtual Environment Workstation Project (VIEW) at NASA's Ames Research Center. Most recently, he has joined with Dr. Brenda Laurel in founding Telepresence Research to continue development of first-person media and applications. Prior to Ames, Mr. Fisher served as Research Scientist with Atari Corporation's Sunnyvale Research Laboratory and has provided consulting services for several other corporations in the areas of spatial imaging and interactive display technology.

Michael Heim, Ph.D., was a Fulbright Scholar for three years in Europe where he studied the cultural impact of technology. His *Electric Language* (Yale University Press, 1987) was the first critical book about the effects of software on literacy. He has just completed another book, *Feedback: Reflections on the Computer Screen,* and was the translator of Heidegger's *The Metaphysical Foundations of Logic* (1984). He lectures in Philosophy at California State University, Long Beach, CA.

Sandra Kay Helsel, Ph.D., is Principal of Infinite Media, a multimedia computer and communications consulting firm. She is editor-in-chief of *Multimedia Review* and chairperson of "Virtual Reality: Theory, Practice and Promise," a conference sponsored by Meckler Corporation. She is author of *Interactive Optical Technologies in Education and Training: Markets and Trends* published by Meckler, 1990. She was Editor, Interactive Videodisc and Multimedia, *Optical Information Systems Update.* Her articles have also been featured in *Instruction Delivery Systems* published by the Society for Applied Learning Technology and *The Videodisc Monitor* published by Future Systems, Inc.

At the national level, she was a member of the Interactive Video Industry Association's planning committee for the Tech 2000 gallery. She has presented at the Sony Videodisc Institute and consults regularly for the Nippon-funded Japanese Language Videodisc series. She spent a year in the electronic publishing industry during which time she was the Senior Project Officer at Intellimation. Dr. Helsel is Publications Chair, Board of Directors, International Interactive Communications Society. She has been active in the formation of a Los Angeles IICS Special Interest Group in the Venture/Santa Barbara area, and has served on the CINDY awards judging panels.

She received her Ph.D. from the University of Arizona on "A Set of Criteria Derived from Curriculum Theory to Assist in the Planning, Use and Evaluation of Educational Interactive Videodisc."

Joseph Henderson, M.D., is Director of the Interactive Media Laboratory (IML) at the Dartmouth Medical School and is active in developing better methods for the presentation and representation of medical information. The IML has three main goals: (1) to develop interactive media programs in health education for users in and outside Dartmouth College, (2) to provide a workshop where educators can learn and use tools for interactive medical development, and (3) to promote the use of interactive media in education through demonstrations, seminars, and a fellowship program. He has designed, written, and produced several award-winning interactive media programs.

Joan Sustik Huntley, Ph.D., is Research and Development Project Leader, Weeg Computing Center, University of Iowa. She directs the Computer-Assisted Instruction (CAI) Laboratory which conducts research and development on the application of new computing technologies in higher education. Since 1978, much of the Laboratory's work has focused on multimedia applications using a variety of development and delivery configurations including videodisc, WORM, and rewritable optical drives on IBM-PC, Macintosh, and the NeXT Computer. She received her doctorate in Instructional Design from the University of Iowa in 1978.

Myron W. Krueger, Ph.D., has experimented with artificial reality since the 1960s. *Artificial Reality* was published by Addison-Wesley in 1983; an updated version was published in 1990. He is President of Artificial Reality Corporation which has developed two operational prototype technologies. One prototype is Videoplace at the Connecticut Museum of Natural History (Storrs, CT). Videoplace visitors in separate rooms can finger paint together, perform free-fall gymnastics, tickle each other, and experience additional interactive events. The other prototype is Videodesk in which hands lay at rest on a desk and appear on the computer screen. Dr. Krueger has a Ph.D. from the University of Wisconsin.

Brenda Laurel, Ph.D., is a self-styled interactivist and has worked in the personal computer industry since 1976 as a programmer, software designer, marketeer, producer, and researcher. Her academic background is in theatre, and she holds an M.F.A. and a Ph.D. in theatre from Ohio State University. Her work on interactive fantasy systems was begun at the Atari Research Laboratory in 1982 and was published in her doctoral dissertation in 1986. She currently works as a consultant in the areas of entertainment software and human-computer interface design for such clients as Apple Computer, Inc., Lucasfilm, and Carnegie Mellon University. She is editor of the new book, *The Art of Human Computer Interface Design*, published by Addison-Wesley Publishing Company (1990) and author of a book entitled *Computers as Theatre*, also from Addison-Wesley, with publication slated for early 1991.

Bret C. McKinney is a consultant and writer specializing in emerging visual communication technology and strategic application management. He has held several positions contributing to the latest HDTV testimonials to the Defense Manufacturing Board, Microelectronics and Computer Technology Corporation, and HD Pacific, a non-broadcast high-definition firm. Currently, he is a consultant to Baylor's New Video Technology Project which specializes in HDTV and peripheral technologies and disciplines. He is author of a book entitled *The New TV: A Guide to High-Definition Television* to be published by Meckler 1990. He has a BA degree from Baylor University in Waco, TX.

Michael Partridge is a Programmer for the University of Iowa's Computer-Assisted Instruction Laboratory. He has over seven years of experience in professional positions in data processing at the University of Iowa Hygienic Laboratory and the University of Iowa Foundation. He has a B.A. in Psychology from the University of Iowa and senior standing in the Department of Computer Science. His interests are in human/computer interactivity, artificial intelligence, and interactive multimedia.

Judith P. Roth has been active in optical storage technology since 1979. She has been involved with write-once optical disk application development and several CD-ROM publishing ventures. Her projects have included the production of an information storage and retrieval videodisc-based spatial data management system for DARPA, design of a videodisc-based electronic retail kiosk and the use of videodisc technology for basic skills education in the U.S. Army.

She is editor-in-chief of *Optical Information Systems,* co-editor-in-chief of *Multimedia Review,* and chairperson of the Annual OIS Conference and Exposition sponsored by Meckler Corporation. She is author of *Essential Guide to CD-ROM, CD-ROM Applications and Markets, Rewritable Optical Storage Technology, Case Studies of Optical Storage Applications,* and *Converting Information to WORM Optical Storage: A Case Study Approach.* In addition, she is co-editor of *Software for Optical Storage* with Brian A. Berg. She has written extensively about optical storage technology in *Popular Computing, Journal of the American Society of Information Science, Library Software Review, AAP Newsletter, High Technology,* and *Educational and Instructional Television.* She has an M.S.L.S. from Syracuse University and attended the Information Systems Seminar at the Sloan School of Management at the Massachusetts Institute of Technology in 1981.

Michael B. Spring, Ph.D., is currently an Assistant Professor of Information Science at the University of Pittsburgh where his research involves the application of technology to the workplace with particular attention to electronic document processing. For more than a decade prior to joining the Department of Information Science, Dr. Spring served as Associate Director and then Director of the University External Studies Program at the University of Pittsburgh. He has authored articles in the areas of office automation, text and document processing, information technology standardization, and educational technology. He has led research projects in the areas of academic electronic publishing, intelligent text conversion and document databases. Currently, he is preparing a book on *The Document Processing Revolution.* He has a B.A. in psychology from the College of the Holy Cross (Worcester, MA) and a Ph.D. from the School of Education at the University of Pittsburgh.

David C. Traub, Vice President of Development, CenterPoint Communications (San Jose, CA) has been involved with multimedia educational computing since the early 1980s. He was a contributor to Microsoft's 1988 *The CD-ROM Yearbook* and *The CD-ROM Handbook* edited by Chris Sherman (Intertext/McGraw-Hill co-publication). He has had articles published in *Optical Information Systems, Multimedia Review, Videography, HyperMedia, Australian MacWorld,* and *Bits and Bytes*

Magazine (New Zealand). He has written a Federal government report comparing six Macintosh-based editing systems for government-directed training development centers. He is an experienced designer and producer of multimedia software and programs for educational application. His clients include Apple Computer, and Encyclopedia Britannica Software. He has an M.A. from Harvard University's Interactive Technology Program in the Graduate School of Education.

Randal Walser is manager of the Autodesk Cyberspace Project. The roots of his interest in cyberspace go back eighteen years, to work on reconstruction of three-dimensional brain models from CAT scans. He went on to work in many areas of AI, and then turned to videogames in the early eighties. As a designer for Bally/Midway, he spent two years developing "Cyber Ridge," a futuristic survival game that mixed 3D graphics with photorealistic 360-degree images. Later, as leader of the TeamWorks Project at Advanced Decision Systems, he focused on coordination and control of telerobotic teams. He joined Autodesk in 1988.

Index